Manifesting Love
From the Inside Out

TAMMI BALISZESWSKI

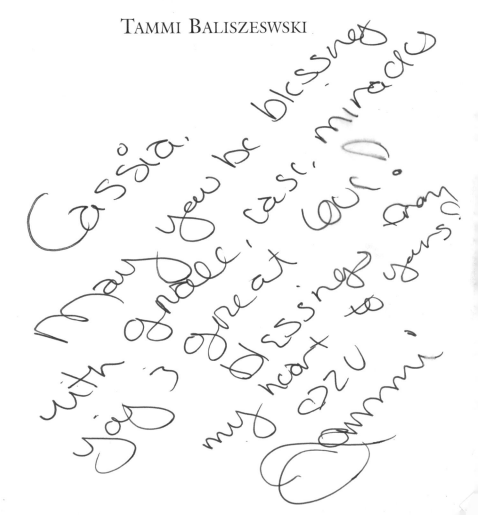

Cassia,
May you be blessed
with grace, ease, miracles
& joy & great case. our !
blessings & love
my heart to yours.
XO U
Tammi

Manifesting Love
From the Inside Out

Tammi Baliszewski

Expanding Heart Publishing
228 E. Plaza St., Suite B. #112
Eagle, Idaho 83616
www.ManifestingLove.net

Copyright 2009

Cover Design: Lily Kovacevic
Book Design: Shawn Beyer

ISBN 978-0-61527-402-7
Printed in the United Sates of America

The Caxton Printers, Ltd.
Caldwell, Idaho

This book is dedicated to Steve, Spirit and all the Souls who are ready for true love!

Contents

Acknowledgments

The creation of this book truly took a village! There are so many who offered their wisdom, stories, thoughts, support, encouragement and love throughout the process.

Thank you, Stephani Jordan, for your kindness and generosity of spirit. You supported me in taking my first baby steps on the path to healing and authentic power.

Thank you to Drs. Ron and Mary Hulnick. Your wisdom continues to ring in my ears to this day. Thank you for creating the wonderful, healing, sacred space called the "University of Santa Monica." I learned to love myself in that building on Wilshire. I have said it before and I will say it again, attending USM was the best gift I ever gave to myself! It is a remarkable program and you are two truly remarkable teachers.

Thank you, Gavin Fry, for supporting me in "processing my stuff" and polishing my book. Your intuition is astonishing and your wisdom profound. You are always there when I need you and I am so blessed.

Thank you to Samantha Fewox. First you cast me in "Baywatch" and helped me get my SAG card, then you taught me about punctuation and helped me edit my book! Thank you for your kindness, diligence, honesty and hard work. But most of all thank you for the gift of your friendship.

Thank you, Linda Humphreys, for combing through my content and making me get into my left brain (even though it was sometimes painful). You have been a beacon of light and a cheerleader of the highest order. I am certain this book would not exist if it wasn't for you. I love you dearly.

Thank you Lily for your diligence in interpreting the art in my head and getting it on to the cover (and on my website!). Not only have you been patient and kind, you have become a friend.

Thank you to my Manifesting Love Sisters, Kathy Ziegler, Sabrina Faith, Noelle Rodreguez, Cynthia Holloway, Penny Malibran, Linda Humphreys and Hadia Haaj. It was a honor to support you and a profound gift to receive your support. You are all earth angels and the wind beneath my wings. (Congratulations on all the engagements!) I love you so much!

Thank you Larry Hickey. Your faith has been unwavering, your intuition astonishing and your support heaven sent. You have been a touchstone, and a wellspring of hope and truth for many years. I am grateful beyond what words can express.

Thanks to all of my dear family and friends who have loved me and been there through the tears and the laughter: Arna Vodenes, Lisa Clapier, Pete Bellon, Natalie Gladwin, Rollene Billings, Tim Greenfield, Gina Deeming, Niki Fretwell, Nikki Cottem, Vina Parmar, Katrina Goodrich, Denise Hendricks, Manna Ko, Jerry Frank, Sunny Jewett, Logan Peel, Carter Peel, Tonda Mason and Mindy Maguire. It hasn't always been easy, but it has always been good!

Thank you to my Mom, Judy Butler. I am so proud of you and am so grateful for your pride in me. Keep up the great work and thank you for loving me unconditionally.

Thank you Mimi, Les and Grammy. I know you are my angels in heaven and loving me even now. I feel your presence everyday.

Thank you to my incredible husband Steve Peel. You believed in this project before I believed in it myself. You have been the greatest blessing of my life and I am so grateful. You are truly an amazing human being and I am honored and humbled by your presence. You are my sounding board, voice of reason, consultant, playmate, best friend and my true love. I adore you completely!

And finally, thank you to Spirit. Thank you for every step that has gotten me to where I am at. Thank you for the blessings I receive daily: the growth, the healing, the synchronicity, expansion and joy. I love co-creating with You and supporting others in realizing Your Presence within themselves. What an amazing journey…and I have a feeling the best is yet to come!

Introduction

Some people pursue happiness, others create it.
~Unknown

We are our own dragons as well as our own heroes,
and we have to rescue ourselves from ourselves.
~ Tom Robbins, American Novelist

As children we were the audience to fairy tales, we were drawn to the magic and believed in it. Prince Charming was the hero, the knight in shining armor who rescued the damsel in distress. In these wonderful stories the prince and princess fall in love and end up living "happily ever after." How can we be blamed if this is what we grow up believing and hoping to achieve in adulthood? But what happens *after* the happily ever after? *There is no sequel!*

If finding the love you desire is frustrating, difficult, painful or impossible, or if you are noticing certain patterns in your relationships you prefer not to repeat, you can greatly benefit from *Manifesting Love From the Inside Out*. It will support you in becoming aware of your core beliefs and what you can do to understand and heal them. This book also can assist you in becoming clear, conscious and empowered in the area of relationships, including the most important relationship of all—the one you have with yourself.

In *Manifesting Love*, relationships are addressed from the "inside out" rather than the "outside in." What that means is, rather than seeking someone special who will complete you, this book will support you in becoming aware and accepting that *you are that someone special—you are already complete!* When you truly accept this on the deepest level, a loving, supportive, sacred partnership can easily and naturally show up in your life.

All relationships reflect what we think, feel and believe. They also reflect our internal sense of value. If you look into a mirror and are unhappy with what you see, it would be useless to get angry at the mirror and draw all over it with crayons or markers. You know that you must take responsibility for your body and its appearance. Once you do, the reflection in the mirror naturally changes. When we choose to heal by taking responsibility for our primary relationship (the one with ourselves), then our life, our experiences and our relationships transform and are reflected back to us in beautiful and remarkable ways.

As a Holistic Life Counselor, I have worked with many clients who face significant challenges with their love relationships. It seems everyone wants to be happy and in love, but the goal is elusive. Many of us seek that "special relationship," but once we think we found it, it's not long before our lives are fraught with drama, confusion and pain.

When you use pure action and willpower to "get" what you want, you are chasing after something that is probably going to elude you in the end. Alternatively, if you are passively waiting for the relationship you desire to show up out of the blue, you can feel disempowered and hopeless. In order to consciously and effectively manifest (in other words, attract or draw forth) what you want, it is necessary to use your thoughts, feelings and the laws of the universe. When we take responsibility for our inner reality—what we think, how we feel, how much we respect and love ourselves—this is what I refer to as "inner work." Inner work not only empowers us, it profoundly changes our lives for the better.

I wrote this book not only because I see my clients struggling with relationships, but because of my own history. My need to become clear in the area of relationships and to heal was put into motion because of my personal devastation, anguish and heartache.

I was courted and romanced by a high profile actor that I'll call Bob. He was sensitive, brilliant and successful. I thought he was my knight in shining armor. The three-year relationship started with incredible promise and romance. As time passed, it started to deteriorate and progressively became more confusing and painful. The relationship ended with me feeling deeply betrayed and abandoned. When I prayed about this reoccurring theme in my life, I began to realize that the pattern continued because I continually betrayed and abandoned myself. My "dark night of the soul" took place in the mid-1990s, and I have devoted myself to understanding myself, healing and becoming whole ever since.

I am now in the most incredible, supportive, respectful, Spirit-filled relationship with a most extraordinary man. People say I'm lucky and I admit that I am. But what people perceive as luck is really a byproduct of healing pain, accepting responsibility, forgiveness, prayers and education in the fields of spirituality and psychology.

Many people have asked me how I got from there to here. I tell them what I have learned: to manifest our beloved, we must first come into a loving relationship with ourselves—we have to understand that *we are the beloved*. Fairy tales have lead us to believe it takes someone else to make us whole and complete, however the reality is that perfect love and "happily ever after" can occur only *after* we become whole and complete within ourselves. Once we do this, we can easily recognize and attract another whole person.

Not everyone has a desire to be in a relationship and that is fine. I am not suggesting that a romantic partnership is necessary for a fulfilling and happy life. However, if you *do* have a desire to be in a loving relationship, I believe you can absolutely bring about that wonderful partner. If you have a genuine interest in attracting true love, this book will provide clarity, encouragement and support.

Throughout this book I refer to God or Spirit. There are many words to describe what is perhaps indescribable—The Creator, The Universe, Buddha, Allah, Nature, Higher Self, Supreme Being, Creative Intelligence, Source or the Divine are some of the names. You may have your own word or way of describing the energy that breathes us. By more fully aligning with this source of wisdom, our lives can take on new and profoundly deeper meaning. Spirituality has been a vital aspect in my healing, my journey to wholeness, as well as the foundation for my beliefs, theories and these writings.

Many of the exercises outlined in this book take courage and strength, as well as a strong commitment. If you apply yourself, you may find that you are stretching out of your comfort zone and into unchartered territory. However, if you are willing to make yourself a priority and show up on your own behalf, you are being presented with a wonderful opportunity to experience revelations, clarity and healing. I assure you, the benefits and rewards for honestly participating in this process will be nothing short of extraordinary.

How to Receive the Most Value from *Manifesting Love from the Inside Out*

Begin keeping a "Manifesting Love Journal." Get a special notebook or journal that you can devote to the practice of manifesting love.

Devote a little time each day to your practice of manifesting love. First thing in the morning or each evening before you go to sleep are wonderful times to do this work. Consistency helps in the process of manifestation.

At the end of each chapter there are a series of questions and exercises designed to anchor the application of the key principles into your relationship with yourself and others. I suggest you complete these end-of-chapter sections in your journal. The more you wholeheartedly participate with this book and these exercises, the more value you will receive in bringing about the love relationship you desire. You may notice some of the exercises seem repetitive or very similar in nature. Each exercise is intended to build on the others, creating an opportunity to deepen your understanding and assist you in accessing greater healing potential.

In addition to doing the exercises, you are encouraged to write any thoughts, feelings, dreams or revelations in your journal. Keeping a journal is an excellent way to anchor what you learn, move energy, keep track of your progress and get to know yourself in a deeper way.

As you read *Manifesting Love* and experience any personal revelations, epiphanies, or "ah ha!" moments, record them in your journal. Consider underlining anything that strikes you as particularly important. Revelations can shift and heal you in an instant. Let your epiphanies add up and support you in manifesting your loving relationship.

Consider partnering with a friend or a group of friends who also desire to bring about a loving relationship. Get together every couple of weeks to share your experiences and journey. Review the exercises at the end of the chapters and support each other. Plan to encourage each other, see the best in one another and lift each other up. Other suggestions might include sending e-mails, making telephone calls throughout the week, sharing success stories, revelations or sending thoughtful cards. Outer support can be extremely powerful when it comes to successful manifestation.

Take what works for you and leave the rest. Everybody's path is different and unique, however, there are common denominators and basic lessons for all of us. I know I have experienced profound and valuable lessons in manifesting respectful, conscious, uplifting relationships. May this book support you in finding yours.

Chapter 1
Relationships as Mirrors

We do not see things as they are, we see things as we are.
~ The Talmud

We meet ourselves time and again in a
thousand disguises on the path of life.
~ Carl Jung

Within most of us is a desire to connect, a hunger for union and a longing for true love. We want someone who will be our lover, our partner and our best friend. Then why is finding love so elusive, challenging and frustrating? Are we too particular? Are we unrealistic? Or even worse, is it simply not our destiny? Although we have been told we are created in God's image, most of us have difficulty accepting our sacredness. For most people, the longing for wholeness and the desire to believe in our innate goodness is worked out in personal relationships.

Buddha told us, "The external world is only a manifestation of the mind itself." In other words, our experience of outer reality is simply a reflection of our inner reality. We all know we can look into a mirror and see the reflection of our physical selves looking back at us. In a much broader sense, our "worldly mirror" reflects back to us, what we think and how we feel. Beliefs, both conscious and unconscious, dictate the quality of our lives. Our income (or lack of it), opportunities, life experiences, how we are treated and our relationships are a few examples that allow us to bear witness to our thoughts, feelings and beliefs.

Relationships, both good and bad, provide the biggest opportunities to observe how we feel about ourselves. If we have a distorted perception of ourselves, we will inevitably see our reflections as misshapen and twisted—similar to what we might see when we look in a funhouse mirror. However, since we accept our perception as the truth, the reflection in the mirror will appear to be real. Relationships can assist us by bringing repressed material to our conscious awareness for the purpose of learning, healing and growth. They will consistently reflect our internal beliefs, perceptions and mis-perceptions back to us.

The Law of Resonance

We attract people through the "law of resonance." We are unconsciously attracted to people who resonate or reflect our issues and beliefs. If you do not love and accept yourself, you will attract people who do not love and accept you. If you constantly criticize and demean yourself, those around you will criticize and demean you. If you betray and break promises to yourself, others will as well. If you always feel like people will abandon you, you set the stage to attract people who will do what you expect them to do. Your inter-nal beliefs are reflected by the law of resonance and, there-fore, create your relationship experiences.

The wonderful thing about the law of resonance is that it gives us the opportunity to gauge how we feel about our-selves. Look at the people in your life and honestly assess how they treat you. Do they treat you with love and acceptance, or do they criticize and demean you? Do they stick with you through difficult times, or do they abandon you when the going gets tough? Do they prize you and lift you up, or do they focus on your negative qualities and put you down? If you pay attention and choose to observe relationships in this way, you will find the people in your life treat you exactly as you treat yourself.

We allow people who reflect our internal beliefs to get close to us. The good news is that if people treat us worse than we treat ourselves, we will either get rid of them or not let them in our lives at all. Conversely, if you do not like or respect yourself and someone comes along who does treat you with honor and respect, he or she probably will not be in your life for very long. When honor, kindness and respect is not an aspect of our "internal environment," these qualities will seem foreign, strange and uncomfortable.

Joe's Story

I have a friend, Joe, who did not respect himself. He would often judge and berate himself. Joe believed the only thing of value he had to offer was money. Consequently, women frequently took advantage of him. When I asked Joe about the value of his love, he did not answer the question. He responded with, "All women care about is money and material things." I tried to help Joe identify and shift his beliefs, but he argued his point. Joe was not ready to do things differently; he was not willing to "go within" and take personal responsibility for his relationship with himself. He told me he would open his mind and change his beliefs only *after* he found one good woman who was not "all about the money."

Joe was pinning his hopes and dreams on something external, rather than taking responsibility for his internal relationship with himself. He wanted his outward experience of life to change before he would change his mind. What he did not understand was that if he would change his mind, his life would follow suit.

If Joe had worked to develop a respectful, loving relationship with himself, he would have had a deeper, more authentic understanding of his innate value and worth. This would have assisted Joe in naturally attracting (and being attracted to) women who also respected and valued him on all levels. However, Joe was not willing to do the "inner work" and remained a victim of his viewpoint. Joe eventually married a woman who was a prostitute. It was his hope that by rescuing her and changing her ways, he would finally validate his worth. Not surprisingly, the marriage did not last and Joe continues his cycle of despair and destruction, with even more "proof" that women are self-serving, conniving gold diggers. True love still eludes him.

The journey to manifesting an authentic loving relationship has to start from within. It is difficult, if not impossible, to authentically love another, or allow ourselves to be loved until we can first love ourselves.

The foundation of all relationships is built on the relationship we have with ourselves. In order to manifest a healthy loving relationship in the outer world, we must first develop a healthy relationship in our inner world. The real purpose of relationships is to let us know how we are doing; to mirror what we think and believe. No relationship is a coincidence. We create them for the purpose of self knowledge and awareness. Relationships give us a wonderful opportunity to observe ourselves and to discover where we may need to work on ourselves. We project both negative and positive attributes on other people all the time. Whether you have a strong positive or a strong negative reaction to someone, it is all ultimately a reflection of yourself.

Exercise: Relationships as Mirrors

1. Open your journal.

2. Think of someone you respect and like.

3. List several of the qualities you admire about this person.

4. Now think of someone you do not like.

5. List several of their qualities that you perceive as negative.

6. Review both of these lists.

Do you recognize these qualities, or the potential for these qualities, from both lists within yourself? By recognizing these qualities, both positive and negative, you are merely witnessing different aspects of yourself. You would not have the ability to identify any quality or characteristic for which you do not have an internal reference point. You would essentially be blind to those qualities and unable to recognize or comprehend them. If you can perceive it, it is a part of who you are. If you choose to hold these people—or any of their qualities—as separate and apart from yourself, then you disown aspects of yourself. This creates a "splintering off" from self; in other words, a disconnection, distance and judgment within yourself and toward others. Living in judgment constricts us and limits our potential. It also diminishes our capacity for authentic connection and happiness.

Exercise: Circle of Friends

1. Turn to a blank page in your journal.

2. Draw a large circle.

3. Put your name in the middle of this circle.

4. On the periphery of the circle, write down the names of the important and influential people in your life (your family, friends, co-workers, boss, etc.).

5. Beside each person's name, write down a few of the qualities and characteristics that first come to mind as you think of each one of them.

The group you assembled is a snapshot of your internal state. Their qualities and characteristics are also *your* qualities and characteristics. How do you feel about your reflection? Are you pleased? Delighted? Embarrassed? Proud? Ashamed?

When I first did this exercise, I was dismayed. I was not all that pleased with my "reflection." I began to wonder why I was spending my time and energy with people whom I was not proud to be identified with and who were not kind to me. I was starting to understand that I was not proud of or kind to me either.

Someone then shared an interesting concept with me: one-third of the people in the world will love you, one-third will be indifferent toward you and one-third will hate you. This was a powerful revelation for me. To me it meant that if you are in a loving relationship with yourself, you will naturally attract those who treat you lovingly. If you do not value yourself, you will spend your time trying to convince those who are indifferent to you that you are worthwhile. If you hate yourself, you will find yourself in harsh, hurtful or abusive relationships.

This information was presented to me at a time when I was becoming aware that I did not particularly care for myself. Many of my friendships consisted of lies, betrayal and inappropriate boundaries. (The question I should have been asking was how did I lie, betray and have inappropriate boundaries with myself?) I started to realize that I was a "people pleaser" and wanted *everyone* to like me. Out of habit, I was spending a great deal of energy on people I did not get along with. I was trying to keep everyone in my life happy; often sacrificing what was best for me. The problem was, in most cases, I was not even sure what was best for me! If asked how I felt about something, I often did not have an answer. I was simply out of touch with myself. However, what I was becoming more clear about was my deep-seated belief that other people were always more important than me.

Significant personal crisis occurred for me at the end of a three-year relationship with Bob, a man I was engaged to. He struggled with addictions and had cheated on me numerous times. When he finally decided to leave me for another woman, I was devastated, confused and distraught. Part of me believed that suicide was the only answer. I decided to pray and asked God why I was always betrayed and abandoned. I suddenly understood it was because I betrayed and abandoned myself. It was a clear, simple and profound truth and I knew this moment of clarity was God's way of answering me.

I had gone along with things I was uncomfortable with, I tolerated situations that hurt me and I was quiet when I should have spoken up. I was afraid of getting in trouble and rocking the boat. I did not really believe I was as important as my partner or that my opinion mattered. I was often quiet and tried to be the "good girl," much like I did as a child. This relationship was reflecting back to me what I believed to be true about myself, men and life. Without knowing it, I had created a self-fulfilling prophecy.

I like the saying, "God throws pebbles, stones, bricks

and then you get a brick wall." We may start to become aware of patterns in our lives that begin with painful little experiences. These "pebbles" can evolve into bigger and more painful experiences and turn into "stones." If we do not learn our lessons, then we get the "bricks." Finally the whole "wall" tumbles down and we no longer have the option to proceed down that path. It seems many of us need to have this brick wall come crashing down before we finally consider going within to heal ourselves.

I had many unsatisfying relationships that seemed to have similar themes of abandonment, cheating and betrayal. When I met Bob, I thought I finally found a good man; he seemed so different than the others. However, I had not done any "inner work" to heal my relationship with myself or my beliefs. In the end, the relationship with Bob was more of the same, but much worse. That relationship ended up being my brick wall. I decided I must be a strong soul indeed, to need something of this magnitude to finally get me to crack. I have heard it said "a nervous breakdown can sometimes be the beginning of a break through" and "sometimes you have to break, before you break open." For me, this was all true.

Universally, crisis and pain are the great awakeners. In Zen teachings it is said that heaven and hell are only a tenth of an inch apart. It is often in the pit of despair and agony that we finally surrender and drop the barriers of our ego. Only when this break through happens can the true radiance of the soul shine through.

After I felt the initial shock, horror and pain of my brick wall, my ego was shattered and I released the pretense of knowing anything. It was time for me to commit fully to Spirit and myself. I had to figure out who I was without a man influencing me and how to stand on my own. I realized if I ever wanted to have a healthy fulfilling partnership, I was going to have to make significant changes. I set forth my clear intentions: to know God, to know myself and to heal.

Exercises: Constricted versus Expansive Beliefs

1. Get out your Manifesting Love Journal.

2. Given that our experience of outer reality is a reflection of our inner beliefs, take a moment to recall a recent situation with a key relationship in your life in which you found yourself getting really upset.

3. Write down the feelings you experienced as a result of this situation (i.e.; hurt, anger, jealousy).

    Example: *I was deeply hurt when my fiancé abandoned me. I was sad, confused and really angry.*

4. Write down what this situation or relationship is reflecting about yourself.

    Example: *He was mirroring to me my belief that I have no value; I do not matter and I do not deserve to be loved.*

    Allow yourself to really *feel* this deep-seated belief that you have just identified, as it may bring up some repressed emotions. It is important to be compassionate and patient with yourself as you begin to walk through this process.

5. As our feelings often flow directly from our deeply held beliefs, take a moment to review and write down some of the *constricted beliefs* that may be contributing to the anger or sadness you are experiencing. By clearly identi-

fying these limiting beliefs, you have the opportunity to shift and release them. If these beliefs are not identified and healed, they will continue to operate unconsciously. This will result in inaccurate perceptions, poor discernment, bad choices and unfulfilling experiences in close relationships.

Example: *I believe that no one will ever love me and I will always be abandoned.*

6. Once you have identified and written down any limiting or constricted beliefs, now consider some *expansive beliefs*. Open your mind to a different way of thinking. Restate the constricted belief to one that opens you up to new, different and more powerful possibilities.

Example: *I am special, unique and deserve to be adored. I am loved and loveable.*

7. Take a moment to visualize and imagine that you are fully stepping into the experience of your new expansive belief. Write down what it *feels* like. How are things different? What does life look and feel like from this perspective?

Example: *I am feeling calmer, relaxed and safe. I feel like I matter. People are treating me with kindness and respect. I am dancing in my own light and joy.*

8. Consider and write down some actions steps you can take to more fully invite, explore and integrate your new expansive beliefs. What are you willing to do and how will you do it?

Examples:

I am acknowledging myself in a positive way and will do so throughout the day.

I am committed to doing things that make me feel happy, more loved and cared for. Like taking a long nature walk with my dog, getting a massage or enjoying a bubble bath.

I will create a list of all of my qualities and attributes that make me special and unique. I will review this list daily.

I will affirm and repeat my expansive belief as an affirmation every morning and every evening.

9. Take a few moments to write a letter of acknowledgement to yourself. It is extremely powerful and very important to be able to acknowledge the steps you are taking as you develop a more loving relationship with yourself.

    Example: *I am proud that I am taking these first positive steps and doing this powerful, healing "inner work." I am looking forward to some wonderful changes both in my inner reality and in my outer life experiences!*

When we take these first few steps to open our minds and expand our way of thinking, we create the space for remarkable changes to occur. By simply considering the *possibility* that things can be different, better and more satisfying, we open up and become available to powerful healing potential. By consciously welcoming new and more expansive paradigms regarding loving relationships, our inner environment starts to shift. This will eventually result in experiencing more fulfilling love relationships in our lives.

The following are some common examples of constricted beliefs I see operating in relationships. Perhaps you can relate to some of them:

Men (or women) are not safe or trustworthy.

Close relationships are filled with pain.

I have little to offer a partner in a committed relationship.

Now here are some examples of expansive beliefs:

Some men (or women) are not safe or trustworthy. However, there are mature, loving people who are dedicated to their own growth and would cherish an open, supportive relationship.

Although I have witnessed and experienced painful relationships in the past, I am fully capable of opening to a loving and respectful long-term relationship.

There is not another person like me anywhere in the world. The unique gifts and loving heart I can share with a partner is priceless. (If you would like, elaborate and capture in writing the unique gifts you can bring to a loving partnership.)

Here are some additional examples of expansive beliefs:

I deserve a "great love."

The world is safe.

I am supported in being all that I can be.

I am wonderful!

I deserve to be adored, cared for, supported and respected.

My opinion matters.

I deserve what I want.

I am important.

As you allow yourself to open to your new expansive beliefs, you start to shift your perspective. This shift will support you in attracting what you want verses what you do not want. By consciously welcoming your new, more expansive paradigms in the area of loving relationships, you create a different relationship with yourself and, therefore, with everyone else in your life. Here is the truth: The gift of your love has profound and significant value and it will *absolutely* be reflected in your life once you accept, embrace and believe in it for yourself!

Chapter 2
Taking Inventory

*Your vision will become clear only when
you can look into your own heart.
Who looks outside dreams, who looks inside awakens.*
~ Carl Jung

If you have 100 tears to cry, 98 will not be enough.
~ Marianne Williamson

Basic psychology teaches us that the foundation of what we believe about life, relationships, money, power and the way the world works is established while we are very young. Beliefs are handed down to us from our parents, which were handed to them from their parents and so on. As we grow older, we react unconsciously to the intellectual programming and emotional childhood wounds that occurred before cognitive thought or reasoning was available to our young minds. Core beliefs are formed from this unaware state and we start to energetically and unconsciously create life experiences. Eventually, patterns start to emerge. We do not usually consider questioning habits, patterns, belief systems or "tribal programming" until life becomes really confusing, unmanageable or extremely painful.

When my life became completely unmanageable, I was ready to give up. It was clear I could not rely on my own understanding. I was ready to admit I needed some big help—

I got down on my knees and surrendered to God. As humans, we have free will and choice. God will not inflict Himself upon us. He is there to support us and guide us, but first we must extend an invitation. I lit a candle and performed my own personal "inviting God in" ceremony. My prayers were no longer by rote; it was time for some authentic communication with the Divine. My prayer went something like this:

Dear God, I am so confused and I am hurting so badly. Please help me. I can't figure anything out and I need your help. Please guide me, direct me, lead me to where you would have me go. My heart is broken and I feel so alone. I just want to be happy. I want to be of service, but I don't know what that means or what to do. I surrender to You. Thy will be done.

Looking Within

As I proceeded to cultivate my relationship with Spirit, I also looked honestly at myself and the patterns in my life. I identified painful and distinct reoccurring themes in my relationships. Some of these patterns included:

Working hard for approval, but never receiving it

Jumping through hoops for crumbs

Being objectified

Lying and deceit

Betrayal

Abandonment

In retrospect, I can see exactly why I ended up in relationships that were bad for me and why I had such negative experiences. My thoughts, my feelings, as well as my conscious and unconscious beliefs had created them! On a very deep level I did not like myself or think I had value. I believed approval and acceptance was something to be earned or worked hard for, but never really attainable. I realize now I was chasing situations, experiences, objects and people in order to avoid myself, rather than *embracing* the experience of being me. I was trying desperately to run away from myself.

Relationships can either distract us from ourselves or help us to look more deeply within ourselves. People who do not like themselves may resist looking within for fear of finding the worst. When this is the case, we will more than likely want a relationship (experiences, hobbies or habits) that will distract us from ourselves. Once we start on our healing path and begin to look within, there may well be a period of digging through the uncomfortable "worms, bats and stinky stuff." All of that "stuff," is simply hurt that needs to be healed.

Facing our unpleasant past experiences and reclaiming disowned aspects of our personalities can bring us face-to-face with vulnerability, pain and our own imperfections. Healing requires us to be honest with ourselves and to examine our dark side—the part of us that we would prefer to keep hidden. However, if we continue to deny the existence of our dark side, then painful dramas and the patterns of failed relationships are likely to repeat themselves in our lives. It is by grappling with our darkness that it can be brought into the light and pain can be transformed into understanding. In this way, suffering can be a powerful catalyst and used as a springboard to self-awareness.

When we consciously claim what we want in life, we are setting an intention. For example, if your intention is to heal, you will potentially have the opportunity to move beyond the alarming contents of your personal Pandora's box, to a place of beauty and wholeness. After all, our very essence is beauty, love and joy. If you knew that there was a huge, beautiful diamond at the bottom of your Pandora's Box, wouldn't you agree it would be worth your effort to dig through the discomfort and pain to get to your diamond?

Choosing to invite God in, sit still with yourself, contemplate childhood hurts and taking inventory of your life can be uncomfortable and emotional. However, it is necessary if you have an authentic desire to make significant changes or to understand why certain patterns repeat themselves. It is important to be able to admit you have made mistakes and some of your behavior or choices may have been imperfect. It is also important to forgive the people who have hurt you, forgive yourself and, if necessary, even forgive God. The process can be confusing and unpleasant.

Most people do whatever they can to avoid pain. Carl Jung, one of the founding fathers of modern psychology, said neurosis is caused by the avoidance of legitimate suffering. Denying our flaws and fears is a psychological division that is actually a means of survival. In therapy, and in the deep healing of ourselves, not only do we have to acknowledge our trauma and pain, we need to re-feel it to heal it and become whole.

By acknowledging and connecting with our early hurts and allowing ourselves to cry the tears we have suppressed or denied we have the opportunity to recover. The tears can move through us, cleanse, shift and heal us.

It is hard to relax into our bodies and experience the present moment until we heal our negative emotions. However, we cannot release these negative emotions until we get into our bodies and allow ourselves to feel them. Accepting and embracing *all* of who we are is crucial to our sense of self. It is also important so that we may have the experience of internal peace, congruence and a sense of spiritual well being.

Some of my personal fears included being weak or wrong. It was important to me to be right, strong and the "good girl." By denying my essential humanness and suppressing a lifetime of grief and anger, I was pretending to be someone other than me—I did not fool many people. The things I was trying to hide and deny about myself were obvious to others. The qualities and feelings I attempted to keep hidden in my Pandora's Box, ended up bulging at the seams and overflowed center stage into my life. What I was resisting was persisting.

I had long forgotten my childhood pain, after all, it was in the distant past. I did not believe it mattered in the here and now, but in fact, the ignored and suppressed hurt was influencing my life from behind the scenes. I was emotionally numb. I felt very little—I was not happy and I was not sad. I was just marching forward through life. Challenging and painful situations began to occur and I resisted shedding tears and allowing myself to experience my feelings. I believed if I allowed a tear to fall, it would mean I was weak; I also feared I may never stop crying. I knew on some level the well of grief was deep and I simply did not want to open the floodgates. In the end, the circumstances of my life became so traumatic and painful, the dam finally broke—I cried, and cried, and cried.

The tears eventually slowed down and it felt as if a ray of light was starting to break through. The grief was softening and, for the first time in years—maybe in my entire life—I took a deep breath. It was a breath that completely filled my lungs and it felt so good. Allowing myself to experience the tears and sadness cracked open the door to freedom. It was my mourning, my journey through the "worms and bats" of my past, that was bringing me back to life. I was cultivating compassion and deepening my relationship with myself. I was doing the internal work I needed to do to become more available to myself and, in turn, available for a deep connection with someone else.

As human beings we all make mistakes. That is part of the human experience. If we continue to judge ourselves and not let ourselves off the hook (consciously or unconsciously), the world will also seem to judge us and not let us off the hook. Identifying the judgments and deep-seated beliefs, reframing them and then remembering the truth about ourselves, can be extremely powerful. It can change the way we think and feel about who we are.

The truth is we are spiritual beings having a human experience and we are perfect in our imperfection. We are not our bodies, minds, thoughts or behaviors—we are our souls. We are here to grow in our capacity to love and experience compassion and it all starts with ourselves.

Accepting Ourselves

Committing to our personal healing is about seeking, finding and celebrating our humanness. When we arrive at the place of accepting ourselves, "warts and all," we relax into a more loving relationship with ourselves. When we reside in the place of peace, contentment, happiness and wholeness within, this naturally draws to us great love. Happiness and wholeness are magnetic; they attract like-mindedness. Where we are within ourselves will inevitably determine who we attract in a relationship and the quality of that relationship.

When we clear out limiting or negative beliefs, we become more fully aligned with Spirit. Once we are in a loving relationship with ourselves and Spirit, the universe becomes a joy-filled place. When we release our fear and hurt, love is what is left. From this place of connection and alignment there is constant communication with the world around us. But first, we have to be honest with ourselves. We have to dig in, identify, allow and release our pain. We need to remove the blocks that prevent the flow of love and prosperity into our lives. It is as if we have to become the compassionate and loving keeper of our bodies, minds and spirits. Once we have accomplished this, we naturally experience synchronicity, support and ease. This is when we are truly ready for a sacred partnership with another human being.

Exercise: Questions to Consider

1. What did you learn about the nature of relationships from witnessing the important people and their relationships around you as a child (i.e.; parents, grandparents, close friends, relatives)?

    Example: *There was a lot of fighting, everyone was angry and unhappy. I learned that relationships are not safe and are filled with pain and anger.*

2. What did you learn about yourself, your value and worth as a child?

    Example: *I felt I was a nuisance, a burden and that I was constantly in the way. I felt like I should not be there and I was a mistake.*

3. Now consider and identify any common themes or patterns you experience in your romantic relationships.

    Example: *There is usually a lot of fighting and pain in my relationships and I am often lied to and abandoned.*

4. Notice if there are any common patterns or themes in your present day relationships that could be reflections

of what you learned as a child about relationships and your value in them. If so what are they?

Example: *There are patterns of frustration, unhappiness, anger and feeling unsafe in my relationships. I can also identify patterns of not feeling very important and having no value.*

We establish beliefs as young children and patterns start to emerge from that unconscious mindset. It can be beneficial to identify and understand what we learned when we were young and what our current belief systems are. When storylines repeat themselves, we feel we have *proof* that this is the way the world works. When you believe "this is just the way relationships are" or "this is the way life is" then *that is* the way life will be for you. For change to occur, you have to open your mind to the *possibility* that life and relationships can be different. Once this new paradigm is accepted, you will notice opportunities presenting themselves reflecting your new belief systems.

Exercise: Identifying and Transforming Core Limiting Beliefs

In the following exercise, you may feel some of the questions asked are repeated from the previous exercise. While this may be the case, the goal is for you to answer the questions from a deeper level of awareness. The more thorough and honest your answers are, the deeper the potential for revelations and healing.

1. Take a few minutes to reflect upon the significant relationships in your life. As you do this, identify any unpleasant or painful themes or patterns that have taken place.

Example: *I recognize a pattern of drawing men to me who initially are enthusiastic and want to be in a relationship. Then when I let them in, they seem to lose interest and leave. I am left confused and feel abandoned and sad.*

2. As you reflect upon this pattern, write down the deeper core beliefs that you may be holding about relationships and about yourself.

    Example of beliefs about relationships: *The constricted belief I am getting in touch with is that I think the world is full of invisible dangling carrots that tempt me but I can't ever have what I really want. I believe I will never get my needs met and no one will ever really love me*

    Example of beliefs about myself: *I guess I am not worthy or deserving of what I really want or need.*

3. Identify some of your deeper unmet needs.

    Example: *The deeper unmet needs I can identify are for steady and unconditional love, genuine reassurance and compassion and for someone who truly loves me*

4. What are some things you can do for yourself now to fulfill some of these needs? Create a list of action steps you can take to care for yourself in ways you have not been cared for in the past.

    Example: *I will buy myself a special heart necklace, (bracelet, puppy, fishing pole, etc.) which will represent a promise to me. I promise to do my best to start loving myself unconditionally and cultivating compassion for myself. I promise to stop abandoning myself and will make myself a bigger, more important priority in my life.*

5   Now imagine how it would feel to give yourself the very things you have longed to receive from other people. Take some time to really explore how this feels. Write down your experience.

Example: *I am allowing myself to feel reassured. I am telling myself the things I wish I would have heard from others. I am "trying on" what it would feel like to be important and loved unconditionally. I feel some sadness, but I also feel optimistic. I feel warm, safe and supported.*

By identifying these deep unmet needs, you have the awareness, opportunity and ability to begin to fulfill them for yourself. By doing this, you will experience a greater sense of inner wholeness. Inner wholeness is the foundation required to create a successful, long-term committed partnership with another person. *Chapter 3, Becoming Whole,* will address key principles and next steps in this process.

At this point, I want to acknowledge you for stepping up to the plate and for taking these first important steps in your healing and manifestation process. Although it may be uncomfortable, the experience can be met with remarkable grace, divine support, revelations and miracles. There is no more important work than the accepting, loving and healing of yourself. Know you are not alone as you journey along this path. Spirit supports you and angels celebrate when you turn inward with the intention of knowing the truth of who you are.

Chapter 3
Becoming Whole

Be really whole and all things will come to you.
~ Lao-Tzu

You are not just a small piece of divine essence that was
created to exist separately. At the level of your soul you
are the whole of Spirit. Your loving relationship to
the Universe is total, seamless and complete.
~ Deepak Chopra

Carl Jung spoke of the evolution of the universe and
how the human spirit always "strives toward wholeness,
completion and consciousness." Inwardly, every human
being is already whole; however, we will feel an internal
sense of deficit or inadequacy if we have ignored, disowned
or rejected parts of ourselves. If we try to fit ourselves "into
a box," go too far in an attempt to please others, or try to
be "normal," we often end up pushing aside important
aspects of our selves. When we attempt to be someone other
than who we genuinely are, we alienate and abandon our
true selves. Living in this state of discord and denial can
cause great discomfort in our lives. Inevitably, these disowned (or unconscious) aspects of our selves will work their
way into the conscious experience via relationships for the
purpose of integration, healing and personal wholeness.

Our love relationships tend to be the most fertile ground for learning. Romantic relationships drive us forward on the journey toward integration, expansion and awareness. Love breaks our hearts and brings us to our knees. In music, poetry, books, legends and myths, love is easily the most common subject matter. Heartbreak is frequent—perhaps even unavoidable—as we evolve and become aware of our wholeness.

Many people express a desire to find their soul mate. Often this desire is driven by unmet internal needs, which they seek to have fulfilled from someone or something outside of themselves. They believe when they find "the one," they will experience peace, joy, as well as sense of connection and completeness. Unfortunately, becoming whole is not as easy as finding our male or female counterpart. However, many of us try and try again before we realize that what we are doing is simply not working.

Sue's Story

"Sue" loves the thrill associated with a new relationship. She pontificates on the wonderful and special qualities her new man possesses. She glows in the infatuation and fantasy of her "true love." Typically, her relationship with "Mr. Right" starts to fail after a few months and she experiences hurt and disillusionment. I have observed Sue's heartbreak and disappointment on many occasions. She has often said to me, "He's not the man I thought he was." This is true; he was a disowned aspect of Sue she thought she had found outside of herself. Basically, Sue was looking for a man with qualities and characteristics that she was not taking responsibility for within herself. I doubt Sue will find her Mr. Right until she is willing to do some inner work that will create her solid foundation and sense of wholeness within.

If we feel incomplete, we will always be searching for someone or something outside of ourselves to fill the emptiness. We may find someone and be satisfied for awhile, but those feelings of unhappiness or discontent eventually return. We tend to blame the person we are with and move on to find someone else. This can continue until we finally take responsibility for ourselves and understand that, while a partner can add spice to our lives, each of us is ultimately responsible for our own experience of joy, satisfaction and fulfillment. No one else can create this reality for us. To think another person can give us happiness, a sense of value and a feeling of completion, is to set ourselves up for the eventual failure of every relationship.

While the first blush of love can indeed be exhilarating and intoxicating, the experience is always temporary. The illusion of romantic relationships is like a mirage in the distance. Once we approach, it often disappears, leaving us feeling lonely, confused and disillusioned. The romantic connection is such a powerful and desired experience because it provides us with a sense of euphoria and oneness. We are given a reprieve from our sense of incompleteness, fear, desire and need—uncomfortable qualities that are simply part of the human condition.

In romantic relationships, our beloved becomes the focal point. He or she becomes the center of our universe and, in essence, our "god." Often unwittingly and unknowingly, we begin to give away our power. Our center is now outside of ourselves—a dangerous place for it to be. When we fall in love we are swept away and no longer on a solid foundation within ourselves. We set ourselves up for heartbreak every time we give our power over to another, think someone else is more important than we are, or love someone else more than we love ourselves. False idols will eventually fall.

It is common and understandable to look for someone who possesses the qualities you believe you lack. For example, some men lack a sense of tenderness, so they look for that trait in women. Some women lack a sense of power, so they tend to search for powerful men. In a situation like this, it's not as if two halves can make a whole—two one-legged people cannot come together and start walking like one normal person!

I frequently see situations in which a woman wants to find a rich man. If a woman does not believe in her own personal power, value and ability to support herself financially, she is more inclined to make a man's financial status her top priority. Instead of looking for a man she is drawn to mentally, physically, emotionally and spiritually, she often ends up limiting herself by searching only for a man of means. Alternatively, it is not unusual for some men to make a woman's appearance their top priority. A beautiful woman can, for some, symbolize an external representation of power and prestige.

Often people tend to be on their best behavior in order to "capture" someone with a special quality they believe they lack within themselves. It is this sense of having an internal deficit that leads them to objectify people—they will size up others to determine if they can be useful in filling their own sense of void.

Other dynamics that often occur are power struggles, the sense of being objectified and not being unconditionally loved. A relationship based on something that is lacking inside is often an unconscious agreement to exchange power. In other words, "I will give you what you *want,* if you give me what I *need.*" In relationships where there is a sense of need or deficit, there will be an imbalance of power at some point. Attempts at control and manipulation will eventually follow. When we experience a lack of internal power it is only natural to try and control people and circumstances outside of ourselves to create a sense of safety. However, a successful, healthy relationship can only happen between equals—two whole, self-loving and self-respecting individuals.

The path to wholeness is a personal journey inward, becoming conscious of and then modifying limiting core beliefs and finally learning to love yourself. Only from this place of internal power and wholeness will a sacred partnership have the solid foundation necessary for authentic connection and true intimacy.

For most of my life I believed I needed to be with a powerful man. I thought I would make him feel like a king and he would make me feel like a princess in return. I also thought if I was with a rich, important and powerful man, I would be important and powerful by association. This worked for awhile—until I noticed that I was being catered to, then stepped on and kicked to the side so others could get to this man! What I was not consciously aware of at the time was that I was searching for my identity and value outside of myself. I also was not aware I had the potential—and ultimately the responsibility—to make myself the princess in my own reality. I needed to cultivate my own internal experience of worth, importance and power.

I spent most of my life trying to prove my worthiness and earn love. I thought if I was pretty enough, nice enough and thin enough, then maybe someone might come along who could love me and make me feel like I had value. This was not highly effective. I did indeed manifest men, but they were men who objectified me—this happened because I was objectifying myself. I felt like an empty box that was wrapped in pretty ribbons and bows, but ultimately had no value. I did not believe my love was a gift, so men reflected that belief back to me over and over again. In truth I was trying to create and experience love from the outside in rather than from the inside out.

Painful Endings

There was a great deal of pain at the end of my relationships. It took me a long time to understand the pain I felt was not really caused by the relationship. Relationships are simply a catalyst, or doorway, that draws out the pain that is already inside. When the dissolution of the relationship with Bob occurred, it felt agonizing, confounding, horrifying and debilitating. However, the pain I experienced at the end of the relationship had actually been buried inside of me all along. That experience simply aggravated my wounds and brought up all of the suppressed emotion I had been carrying for a lifetime.

Codependent relationships (as well as all addictions) progress to the point where our pain becomes debilitating and we hit rock bottom. In Zen teachings there is a belief that spiritual growth involves the experience of a red hot coal in our throat that we can neither cough up nor swallow. This means we have to surrender and accept *what is*—we no longer have the option or ability to run from ourselves and our pain.

From the perspective of the soul, our most significant problems and most profound hurts are also our most powerful healing opportunities. As we journey forward on the path to greater consciousness, we often encounter events, people or experiences that bring up hurt in such a way we think we cannot go on. These are opportunities for personal evolution, to invite Spirit in, to become more aligned, more authentic and ultimately whole.

Thornton Wilder, a three time Pulitzer Prize winner, wrote: "Without your wounds where would you be? The very angels themselves cannot persuade the wretched and blundering children of earth as can one human being broken in the wheels of living. In love's service only the wounded soldiers can serve." When we heal, we do not heal alone. By taking personal responsibility for our wholeness not only do we find our way home, we become a beacon of light and a guide to others.

Accepting Your Wholeness

Becoming whole first requires the awareness that perhaps you do not believe you are already whole. Some qualities that indicate opportunities for healing in the area of wholeness are:

Having a sense of loneliness

Taking on too much responsibility

Not taking enough responsibility

A deep sense of not belonging

Masking your emotions

Believing that finding the right lover will complete you

Having significant self doubt

Feeling inadequate

Experiencing significant challenges with boundaries

Judging yourself or others

Feeling profound guilt or shame

Some qualities that indicate a sense of wholeness are:

Valuing and respecting yourself

Maintaining healthy boundaries

Knowing your strengths and weaknesses

Allowing yourself to be vulnerable

Cognizant of your feelings

Feeling comfortable in your skin

Making self-honoring choices with ease

Knowing how to take care of your personal needs

Loving yourself

As you review these lists, can you relate to any of these qualities, characteristics or experiences? Are you whole or are you looking for a piece of your puzzle somewhere outside of yourself? Ask yourself why you want a relationship. Are you lonely? Bored? Is it because you want or need something? Is it because you have something you would like to give? Are you in deficit or do you have an abundance that you would like to share? Do you love yourself and your life? Or are you looking for someone who will give you a greater sense of value, meaning, direction and purpose?

Becoming whole is a process. Although it can require some work, it will ultimately pay off in many ways. When we come to understand that our true source of power is *internal* and *eternal,* we are no longer the walking wounded hoping someone will come along and appease, soothe or complete us. We believe in ourselves and in our place in the world. We also truly enjoy the experience of being who we are.

I have done a great deal of personal healing and I feel I am at last "whole unto myself." Life looks so much different from this perspective. I am no longer anxious and depressed. I am not in deficit, nor am I a wounded victim with a tragic story. Certainly I still deal with the ups and downs of life and I experience moments of sadness, anger and frustration, but I am now living with a greater sense of connection and happiness. I have more experiences of joy and laughter. I am treated with greater respect and honor because I finally respect and honor myself. I am constantly deepening in the understanding that my outer reality is literally a reflection of my inner reality.

Exercise: Embracing My Wholeness

Answer the following questions in your journal:

1. What is it you want from the other person in your relationship? Be specific and create a list of eight to ten qualities or characteristics of your ideal mate.

   Example:

   Qualities I want in a partner:

   A conscious relationship with God
   Physically fit
   Financially stable
   Loves and adores me
   Courageous

2. Review your list. Which of these qualities have you established in a strong way with yourself? Give two or three examples of how you express each quality with yourself.

   Example:

   My strong personal qualities:

   I have a conscious relationship with God.
   a) I pray and meditate every morning
   b) I read books about spirituality
   c) In my journal, I express gratitude to Spirit for all of my blessings on a daily basis

   I am physically fit.
   a) I work out 3-4 times a week
   b) I eat healthy foods and take good care of my physical body
   c) I am consciously grateful for my body and my health

3. Now take an honest look at the qualities and characteristics you want in a partner that may be less developed in your relationship with yourself. Write them down. These less developed qualities may reflect deeper, unmet needs that can be primarily satisfied through deepening your connection with yourself and Spirit.

Example:

Less developed personal qualities:

I am not financially stable
I do not love and adore myself
I do not feel particularly courageous and strong

4. Consider why you desire these qualities in a partner. Get specific and write down two or three examples of how you can take greater personal responsibility for cultivating each of these qualities more deeply within yourself.

Example:

I desire a partner that is financially secure, because I do not believe that I can cultivate prosperity on my own. I am now aware of and setting the intention to take responsibility to challenge and support myself in bringing forward my own wealth of creativity, gifts and financial security.
   a) Meet with a financial adviser
   b) Develop an investment savings plan
   c) Develop a budget
   d) Create a vision board or collage symbolizing my personal prosperity

I want to be loved and adored, but I realize that I do not love and adore myself on a deep level. My intention is to cultivate a more loving relationship with myself so that I may attract someone who also sees and values my wonderful, unique and special qualities.

    a) Enjoy a good book (this book) while soaking in the tub

    b) Treat myself to a nice dinner

    c) Take sunset walks along the beach

    d) Get massages

I want a courageous partner, so I am choosing to take courageous action on my own behalf. I am going to sign up for a class (art, kick boxing, acting, etc.) that I have been considering that I know would uplift me and enhance my growth.

    a) Enroll in an acting class

    b) Take up kickboxing

    c) Join Toastmasters (public speaking club)

    d) Join a dating service

5. Take a few moments to imagine how accomplishing these goals will feel. How does it feel to stand more fully in your own power? Write down your experience. By visualizing, writing and implementing your action steps you are powerfully cultivating, acknowledging and claiming your wholeness.

Example: *I feel very proud of myself! I feel powerful and empowered. I feel optimistic, strong and joyful! I am getting excited about my life and about being me!*

6. Finally, take a few moments to close your eyes, center your awareness in your heart and ask yourself, "What else can I do that will support me in becoming more whole?" Write down the information that comes to you.

Example:

Engage in an ongoing counseling relationship

Make a list of activities that bring me joy and that are deeply nourishing as part of my ongoing "courtship" with myself (Perhaps you can make this a chapter in your journal)

Treat my body with the utmost respect and care with nourishing foods and a fitness routine that I would enjoy

Start a meditation practice

Treat myself to a movie that I have been wanting to see

Although you may not always feel like it, you have a direct connection to Spirit. It is important to become consciously aware that *you are whole and complete!* Understanding, cultivating and owning your wholeness is a vital step on your journey to a deep sense of personal fulfillment. This is also the catalyst that will draw to you a sacred partnership and the love of your life.

Chapter 4
Loving Yourself

To love oneself is the beginning of a life long romance.
~ Oscar Wilde

You, yourself, as much as anybody
in the entire universe deserves your own love and affection.
~ Buddha

The world will always respond to how you feel about yourself. If you hate yourself, then the world will be harsh. If you love yourself, then the world will love you back. I believe coming into loving relationship with oneself is one of the most important journeys we can make and the most powerful lesson we can learn. In fact, I believe it is the primary purpose of our lives. Most of us desire to manifest a supportive, loving relationship. However, to attract that authentically sacred relationship, we must be able to relax and reside in the place of loving within.

Of course we can manifest relationships without loving ourselves, but they do not remain joyous for long. Depending on how much we dislike ourselves, they can become downright excruciating. Relationships can indicate how far off track we have gotten and how much we do not care for ourselves. Any relationship that is not based on a solid foundation of two individuals who love themselves is inevitably going to become a codependent one. If you are not in a loving relationship with yourself, you will attract another person who is not in a loving relationship with themselves. It is similar to building a house on sand. Although the house may look wonderful, it will all come tumbling down when the foundation shifts.

The essence of a spiritual path is learning about love. Every spiritual master—Jesus, Buddha, Muhammad, Krishna, Amma and others—is a messenger of love. Loving others and being of service is the easy and natural by-product of a connection with Spirit and the experience of Self-love. When we are in a loving relationship with ourselves we share from a place of joy and abundance. Most of us have heard the saying, "You can't love someone else until you love yourself." It's one of those simple yet profound messages that continue to grow in depth and meaning as I venture forward on my healing path.

As babies and young children, love seems to occur naturally, spontaneously and joyfully, for love is the essence of who we are. As life unfolds, most of us experience hurt, disappointment and disillusionment. We begin to believe something must be inherently wrong with us and we do not deserve to be loved. The natural loving connection we have with ourselves begins to deteriorate.

Gershen Kaufman, a noted psychiatrist, calls the bond of love and trust between two people the *interpersonal bridge*. As children, we might do something that delights mother or father on one day and, because they are tired or overwhelmed, the same behavior annoys them on the next day. This can be not only confusing, but create a profound sense of helplessness, fear and distrust. Children have a limited understanding of the world, so when trust is broken it can be devastating. At some point, all children experience the collapse of this interpersonal bridge with their caretakers.

When a child does not get the approval and love they desire they wonder, "What is wrong with me?" Many come to the conclusion they are unlovable.

When the interpersonal bridge is broken, the natural side effect is shame and self judgment. It is the rare adult that has maintained a true and positive sense of value and self worth. Most of us have to do significant work to rebuild our interpersonal bridge and come back into "right relationship" with ourselves and the world.

Self-Love

When I speak of Self-love, I capitalize the *S* to represent the fact that every one of us is an aspect of Spirit. We are not just our small selves, our egos, competitive nature and judgments. Each of us is an extraordinary, unique and beautiful face of God. However, most of us are challenged in remembering, accepting and embracing this truth.

Many of us have been taught to put others before ourselves. Kindness, compassion, generosity and thoughtfulness are obviously wonderful attributes, but these qualities will never be completely authentic if we do not cultivate them for and within ourselves. Some believe that Self-love is egotistical and selfish. If someone is boisterous, arrogant or narcissistic, it is not Self-love they are exemplifying. Those qualities are invented by the ego and are smoke screens designed to cover up insecurities and perceived internal deficits.

Self-love is quiet, patient and kind; it is the ability to see oneself from a higher perspective—from the vantage point of angels or Spirit. Self-love is treating yourself with the respect you would extend to a cherished friend. It is the experience of adoration, pride, kindness, affection, amusement and humor toward oneself—even (and maybe especially) when you make a mistake. It is simply accepting yourself completely and unconditionally. Self-love is a unifying experience. It is choosing to believe in your worth, value and ability to be loved despite any and all evidence to the contrary.

Self-love is an inclusive experience; no part of yourself is abandoned, cut off or thought to be bad, wrong or evil. You do not judge yourself; therefore you are not inclined to judge others. There is a prevailing sense of compassion and respect for you and everyone you encounter. The experience of love becomes more open and free-flowing. If someone truly resides in the place of loving within, they are available for an authentic connection with the waiter, the clerk, the telemarketer and the homeless man. There is the deep realization that we are all from the same energy and that energy is love.

If you truly love your Self, your actions, words and deeds do not exclude anyone else's well-being. Your interest is truly about the highest good for all concerned. If you love your Self, you live in harmony with the world. Certainly it can be challenging to maintain this sense of connection consistently, but with intention and practice we are able to string more and more of these moments together.

Internationally known social psychologist, psychoanalyst and humanistic philosopher, Erich Fromm, describes love as an art that requires effort, knowledge and practice. It is a conscious choice and not something we do just once. If we have a past pattern of negativity, it is easy to slip into our old constricted ways while under pressure. Loving our Selves is a moment-to-moment choice. We know we are slipping out of our Self-loving connection when we feel impatient, fearful, angry, judgmental, jealous or annoyed. If this should happen, it is important not to berate yourself. It is better to simply notice your reaction and become aware that you have a choice. One choice might be to say to yourself,-

"Interesting, I guess I am not in the place of Self-love." Another might be to say, "Thank you for this moment" and relax into the space and comfort of the love that exists within. Another option may to simply acknowledge, allow and express your negative emotions and choose to love your Self anyway.

We become truly capable of loving another when we can finally love and value ourselves despite our imperfections and mistakes. We also are more capable of discernment in our relationship choices. If we respect and love ourselves, we never allow anyone to disrespect or abuse us.

When you love your Self, you are better equipped to love others in the right proportions and right ways. When we love our Selves, we see our lives from a much clearer perspective. We are in touch with our feelings, needs and desires. We also know that we are ultimately capable of fulfilling them ourselves. Relationships are no longer based on a sense of need; they are based on a sense of desire. They have clear boundaries and are balanced, positive and uplifting.

Although I have been working on cultivating a loving relationship with myself for quite some time, it seems the subject is always up for review. I had an intensive course in Self-love one week when I backed my husband's SUV into a car causing a few thousand dollars worth of damage, missed a plane to an important meeting, got stood up by some friends and had an allergic reaction to some food that caused my face to puff up and my eyes to swell shut. While on my way to the airport to catch another flight, I realized I forgot my purse, which caused significant grief to my mother and sister who had to help get it to me before my plane's takeoff (which I almost missed again). When I finally made it home, it appeared I had forgotten to pay the cable bill so it was disconnected and my husband could not watch his beloved Boise State Broncos. To top off this wonderful week, I gained five pounds!

As every mishap occurred, I reminded myself that I had a choice. I could either judge, criticize and berate myself for being an idiot or I could accept that I am a fallible human being trying to do my best and making some mistakes along the way. I chose the latter. Although it was challenging, I maintained my connection to Spirit and my sense of worth. My husband was annoyed with me, my sister and mother were also irritated, my head was the size of a watermelon, some business deals had fallen through, my friends had totally blown me off and I felt chubby! Despite all the evidence to the contrary, I chose to believe that God loves me, cherishes me and even finds me adorable and amusing. I consciously and consistently saw the fork in the road with every difficult situation, and I chose to take the high road by maintaining my connection to Spirit and loving myself.

Pain, fear and loneliness occur when we negatively judge or withdraw our approval from ourselves. If you can love and accept yourself despite your imperfections and life's difficult circumstances, you will experience a greater sense of freedom, connection and peace.

Lynn's Story

I was recently visiting Lynn, a wonderful friend. She was in great distress. The relationship with her boyfriend, Scott, had been challenging for the last couple of years and was getting much worse. Lynn was feeling very confused, frustrated, disrespected and unloved. She asked me what I thought she should do. I told her it seemed she was looking for her validation, acceptance and the experience of love to come from her boyfriend. She said, "That's what boyfriends are supposed to do." I told her I thought perhaps she could consider the possibility of validating, accepting and loving

herself. Her response was (which is quite common), "Ewww gross! I don't want to do that! It's easier for me to love Scott!" My response was, "And how is that working for you, Miss Lynn? How is anybody going to see your value if you don't believe you have any?"

Have you heard the saying, "treat others the way that you want to be treated?" I would like to expand on that philosophy by saying: "treat yourself the way you want other people to treat you." Remember, our relationships are our mirrors. How can a person who has an internal environment of disgust, disapproval and general disregard for themself expect a reflection of respect, acceptance and unconditional love? It cannot happen; mirrors simply do not work that way.

To see a reflection of love, one must first have the internal experience of love. Lynn ended up admitting that perhaps her fear and self-loathing were affecting the relationship. She began to realize that *she* was going to have to start being her relationship priority—not her boyfriend. By the end of the conversation, Lynn had committed to taking a few small steps in the direction of Self-love.

The Journey to Self-Love

So how exactly does a person begin the journey of Self-love? As with anything, it begins with awareness, intention, commitment and action steps.

Awareness. In order to change something, we first need to become aware that it needs changing. In order to come into a more loving relationship with oneself, one must first realize there is the possibility and opportunity to come into a new and more positive relationship with oneself.

Intention. By setting your intentions, you set universal

energy into motion. You create a goal in which you will be divinely supported in achieving. (Chapter 16 goes into more detail about the power of intention.)

Commitment. On the journey to Self-love, we must sincerely commit to Spirit and ourselves. We must vow to be courageous and diligent while establishing a more honoring and respectful relationship with ourselves.

Action steps. It is helpful to identify things you can do to show Self-love and then follow through. How can you be kind to you? Some examples might include a getting pedicure or a massage, giving yourself permission to take a nap when you are tired, staying in a hotel and ordering room service, spending time in nature or taking yourself to a movie.

If you are ready to cultivate a more loving relationship with yourself, consider making this Loving Commitment (or you may create a personal vow using your own words). Either write it down and sign it, or say the following statement out loud:

> *I, (your name), am ready to commit to a loving relationship with my Self. I am ready and willing to do whatever it takes to come into an aligned, sincere loving relationship with my Self. I am worthy and deserving of my love, respect and unconditional positive regard. I now promise to love, honor and cherish myself in joyful times and challenging times, now and always. (Sign your name)*

Once you make this loving commitment to yourself, you start to build a solid foundation within yourself. This creates an opening for new opportunities and experiences to present themselves in your life. As you cultivate new habits of supporting and loving yourself, not only will you feel different,

you will find the world starts to treat you differently. Because everything in the world is your mirror, the image in the mirror changes as you change.

Exercise: Tools to Cultivate Self-Love

1. In your journal, write a love letter to yourself. As I mentioned in the introduction, writing your thoughts in a journal is a powerful way to anchor intentions, explore yourself, track changes and to create a deeper sense of connection to Spirit and Self.

2. Create a chapter devoted to Self-love, with the first page of this chapter consisting of your personal commitment to yourself.

3. Set an intention to honor yourself and be kind and patient with yourself even when you make mistakes. Treat yourself with patience, gentleness and sweetness. Treat yourself like someone you adore.

4. Practice seeing the good in yourself and all around you. Write down your qualities, characteristics and attributes that you appreciate. List and describe all the things that make you wonderful, unique and special!

5. Respect and adore your body. Make choices that honor and exemplify your respect and appreciation. Your body is the sacred vehicle for your soul and ideal for your learning. Set an intention to appreciate and cherish your body. Create a list of things you like or appreciate about your physical self and how it serves you. Consider things you can do to cultivate and deepen this loving relationship with your body.

6. Before you go to bed at night, write down as many things as you can think of for which you are grateful and why. Remember, the things we focus on expand. By focusing on the good in your life, you invite in more good.

7. Praise yourself. Criticism breaks us down; praise builds us up. Even with the same sunlight and water, plants in an environment of loathing, criticism and negativity wither, while those that are loved and appreciated flourish. Write down a few things that make you really proud of yourself in terms of who you are and what you do.

8. Create a Self-loving affirmation that you can easily commit to memory. Set an intention to repeat it to yourself several times throughout the day.

Examples:

I am healthy, I am whole and I am in loving relationship with my Self.

I am living a Self-honoring, Self-loving, joy-filled life.

I am a unique, wonderful, divine expression of God and I am lighting up the world with the gift of my love.

I love my Self and I love being me!

In the creation of your Self-loving affirmation, you may want to start with a catchword (or two) that resonates for you and build your affirmation around it. I personally had deep-seated issues of insecurity so a catchword I used in some of my early affirmations was *confidence*. One affirmation I used was: "I am confident and courageous and in a loving relationship with me." It can be beneficial to include *Self-love* in this affirmation. Even if

you do not feel like what you are affirming is true, repeating it will eventually have a positive affect. The words have a power that can shift your focus, beliefs, perspective and experiences.

9. Take a few moments to put this all together. Imagine what it would *feel* like to be in this more supportive and loving relationship with yourself. What does life *look* like from this new perspective? How are things different?

10. List action steps you can take *now* to show kindness, love and appreciation for yourself.

Additional Keys for Loving Your Self

Choose to focus on the positive in life and in yourself rather than the negative. Find the bright side of all situations. Consider any current challenging dynamics and what the possible good is and what the higher learning might be. This is an extremely valuable practice. This is how we stay connected to Spirit, open to financial abundance and receive healing. Focusing on the postive is how we create grace, flow and synchronicity in our lives.

Pay attention to your inner voice. If you find it is being critical or negative, say "no thank you," and then redirect your focus. You would not allow someone to be critical and mean to someone you love, would you? Make a commitment to yourself to say and think kind, uplifting and loving things. What are some positive messages you can share with yourself right now?

Another powerful exercise is to simply look at your reflection in the mirror and connect with yourself through your eyes. Compliment yourself; tell yourself you are worthy, loveable and deserve all your hearts desires. This is also a good time to say your Self-Loving Commitment and affirmations out loud. If you are ready, release any unloving judgments you have against yourself and promise that you will be more kind from now on. Although this can seem uncomfortable or strange at first, it has great potential to assist you in healing and creating a more loving relationship with your Self.

I am reminded of the quote, "If you could see yourself as God sees you, you would be astonished by your beauty!" Each one of us is greater than we realize. There is a potential within you—the potential to claim the extraordinary expression of God that you are. I believe peace, fulfillment and our greatest joy comes from saying yes to the adventure of joyfully discovering and exploring our unique human expression. So, the truth is, *your very essence is exquisite, special, beautiful and brilliant!* When you understand and accept this, you will be amazed by how extraordinary and supportive life can be. Claim your place in the world, claim your value and claim the love that is you with the following statement: *I am an incredible and beautiful expression of God and unique in all the world! I am loved and loveable and worthy of all of my heart's desires!*

Chapter 5
Are You Ready for Love?

In our imaginations we believe that love is apart from us.
Actually there is nothing but love, once we are ready to accept
it. When you truly find love, you find yourself.
~ *Deepak Chopra*

There was a time when the risk to remain tight in a bud
was more painful than the risk it took to blossom.
~*Anais Nin*

Are you really ready to be in a relationship? When you
think about manifesting a relationship do you feel happy,
excited and expectant or do you feel some trepidation? Are
you afraid of feeling trapped or worried that you might be
hurt or disappointed?

Romantic partnerships inevitably lead us back full circle
to our first relationships—the ones with our parents. The
dynamics that occur early in life are the ones we tend to
recreate. Sigmund Freud, an Austrian physician who developed psychoanalysis, referred to this as the *repetition compul-
sion*. It is as if we have unconscious radar that leads us to
what is familiar, even if the familiar is not positive. Children
of alcoholics tend to attract alcoholic mates; children who
were abused find themselves in abusive relationships as
adults. If you were neglected and dismissed, you will strug-

gle to get the attention and affection you desire from your partner. Consider your experiences as a child: Were you given plenty of love and affection or were you ignored? Were you smothered or were you given too much space? Did you live in a strict household or was there a lot of freedom? Consider what the most important relationships in your childhood felt like. What was your relationship like with your mother and father? What about your relationships with other relatives or close friends? What were some of the qualities of those early connections? We all unconsciously tend to recreate what is familiar.

Dueling Intentions

When we are unclear and conflicted about what we really want, we create dueling intentions (also known as mixed messages). Dueling intentions can be somewhat challenging and perplexing. We may have a conscious intention and believe we desire something, but we might also have a subconscious fear of it actually showing up. Many people have a fear of failure, but often those same people unconsciously have a greater fear of success. We may consciously believe we want more money, power, a relationship or to be thin but, at the same time, we may have unconscious fears about how these things could negatively affect our lives.

Subconscious beliefs or fears are an attempt to keep us in our safe zone. Most people fear change and being out of control (Fear and control are the biggest addictions and illusions we have as humans). If we say we want more money or a relationship, but also fear having those things, they will not easily come to us. These contradictions are a way we unconsciously sabotage the manifestation of the very things we say we want. It helps to identify both what we want and our competing intentions. By identifying our roadblocks (resistance or fear), we can work to remove them—*if we really want to.*

Our thoughts and emotions create an energy (or vibration) that brings tangible and intangible results. Our words, thoughts, feelings and actions all create a ripple effect in the world and act like a magnet to attract people, opportunities, objects and situations into our lives.

Whether we want something too much or not enough, the energy we emit prevents it from easily showing up in our lives. When we want something very badly and do not believe we can have it, we often experience an energy of fear and desperation around that desire. Fear acts as a deterrent and can repel the object, goal or outcome.

We all want a sense of freedom, joy and creativity. None of us want to feel trapped, suppressed or controlled. Many of us have had unpleasant experiences in relationships. This can color our outlook and create a vibration that will set us up for recreating other unpleasant relationships. All this unpleasantness may make us think we do not want to be in a relationship at all, but that does not feel fulfilling either. We need to examine these mixed messages and the core beliefs beneath them. Once we acknowledge, understand and release our internal contradictions, we can consciously take steps to become more integrated and congruent.

When we do not admit what we want and consciously claim it, we are much less likely to attract it. This can happen when we do not want to get our hopes too high, or set ourselves up for disappointment. We stand on the periphery rather than in the center of our power as conscious creators. When we are clear about the desire for love, remove the obstacles and claim it, love will find its way into our lives.

It is impossible to manifest true love without an open and available heart. Unresolved pain can be a substantial roadblock. Heart connections that have not been severed can keep you attached to the past, connected to another and energetically unavailable. It is important to clear the pain and heal past hurts if you want to attract your sacred partnership.

For a period of time in my life, I was *saying* that I wanted to be in a relationship; however, I noticed I was consistently attracting men who were emotionally unavailable. I eventually had to ask myself, *why?* The answer was because unconsciously, I too, was emotionally unavailable. You could say I had a foot in and a foot out of the whole relationship thing. I had a fear of commitment and I had not healed my hurt from past relationships. Once I became aware of this, I chose to work with my beliefs and release my fear. I set an intention to become more emotionally available to Spirit and myself. I made a commitment to work on my relationship with myself. This included keeping track of my thoughts and progress in a journal, participating in therapy, studying the teachings of spiritual psychology, meditation and prayer. Only after I took responsibility for the relationship with myself and God and healed my limiting beliefs, did an emotionally available man come my way.

What comes to mind when you consider the word "commitment?" How does it make you feel? Where do you feel it in your body? Is there any negativity or discomfort? Do you contract or do you expand? If you experience discomfort or constriction, be willing to explore it, communicate with it and get to the core of your fears.

Protection from Intimacy

Another dynamic I observe happening in the lives of my clients and friends (and have been guilty of myself), is an attraction to inappropriate people. For example, many women have a fascination with "bad boys." They find them exciting, adventurous and perhaps a little dangerous. In contrast, "nice guys" can seem dull and a little boring. This dynamic is a way of keeping us from an authentic connection and intimacy.

I recreated a pattern from my childhood and was drawn to men that paid little or no attention to me, which fed my thrill of the chase. If a man was slightly disapproving, my attention would be piqued. Unconsciously, I was attracted to people like my father who expected me to jump through hoops for crumbs. I was familiar with emotional abuse and although I did not consciously like it or intentionally seek it out, it was my comfort zone.

These relationships mirrored what I believed to be true about myself—I did not have much value. However, I thought if I worked really hard I could convince a man I was special. Metaphorically, I would play games, put on a mask, juggle and even tap dance for him. Consciously, I thought I was ready for a relationship, but subconsciously I certainly was not ready for love. I had the potential to become infatuated, attracted and intrigued, but I was nowhere near ready for an authentic, mature partnership. I would not have been able to tolerate a loving, respectful and responsible man. If he was too kind, it made me nauseas. I was unfamiliar with unconditional love and did not love myself; therefore, I was uncomfortable and ultimately incapable of accepting love.

As I embarked on my healing path, a teacher asked me about the dynamics of the primary relationships in my early life. It eventually became apparent I was recreating the same experiences I had as a child. My father was not really emotionally or physically present and he was not amused with having three girls under his feet all the time. He was a young, handsome, ambitious military man who was determined to make his place in the world. I was always trying to get his attention and earn his approval which was ineffective. Instead of being seen and treated as the cute loveable girl I truly was, I was treated as a nuisance. Mom was often overwhelmed and would ask my sisters and me to go outside and play. We all longed for her attention, but she did not have the energy, patience or the desire to interact with us. In retrospect, many of the relationships I was having in my adult life were recreating the very same experiences of my childhood—feeling ignored, feeling unimportant and feeling like a nuisance.

Frustration, anger and annoyance were also common threads in my attempts at love. After my parents' bitter divorce, the addition of a strict, angry, controlling, workaholic stepfather made life even more complex. He expected us to be subservient, obedient and hard working. Later in life, I manifested relationships with possessive, angry, controlling men who disregarded my opinions and feelings. My "job" was to behave and be subservient. Again, I was unconsciously recreating what was familiar.

I finally decided to take a look at my patterns and habits in relationships. Some of them included playing games, being coy and flirting to get the attention and approval of men. I also heavily relied on my physical attributes to get noticed. Once I became aware I was doing this, the behavior started to shift. While I was working on cultivating a more committed, respectful, loving relationship with myself, I was preparing for a committed, respectful, loving relationship with a man. Once I became conscious of my deep-seated patterns and beliefs and set my intention to heal, life started to naturally shift. I started to give up the roles I had known for a great deal of my life—no more "good girl," no masks, no games. I decided I wanted to get to know me and be me—all of me—whatever that was. I had nothing left to lose. It was time to give being the *real me* a chance.

Ready for Love

Being ready for love is much more than simply looking good, being witty or playing games. It is more than the process of capturing another or being captured. It is also more than romance, impressing or being impressed. Being truly ready for love is the authentic desire to know yourself, taking full responsibility for yourself, living in your truth and honoring yourself. It is the desire to become honest and real and to connect with another person who is coming from the same place. This is the fertile ground where vulnerability and intimacy can begin to take root. This is the foundation where the seeds of true love are sown. When we set the intention for love in our lives, we give up a certain amount of control. Where there is real love, there is no need or desire to control.

Negative experiences from past relationships can linger in many ways. Unpleasant memories and judgments based on these memories can affect your current beliefs about relationships and limit your ability to live in joy. When looking back on your past relationships, focus on the gifts they gave you. Ask yourself, "What did I learn? Where were the blessings? What about the relationship was good and positive?" By choosing to focus on the positive aspects of so-called failed relationships, we redirect ourselves, shift our vibration and attract more positive relationships and experiences in our lives.

By consciously choosing to redirect our focus to the more positive aspects of past relationships, we can soften our anger, hurt and frustration. We can start to see things from a higher altitude. This can shift our vibration and what we will attract in the future. Whatever we choose to focus on will expand. When we observe, discuss, think about and focus on the negative we call forth more negativity. By choosing to observe, discuss, think about, or focus on the positive, we call forth more positive.

Focusing on the negative aspects of being in a relationship leads to constriction and limitation. Loss of freedom was one of my fears about being in a relationship. This fear brought possessive, controlling and jealous men into my life and I felt trapped. When I focused on observing other peoples' relationships in which there appeared to be mutual support, respect and freedom, I came to realize that freedom is an inside job. I could not manifest a relationship where I felt safe and free, until I had the sense of safety and freedom within myself.

Another limiting belief I held was that relationships always entail pain and compromise; after all, this had been my experience since I was very young. I worked hard to heal the pain and disappointment of my Inner Child, which helped me to move past these beliefs. I opened up to the possibility that my future relationship would not entail pain, compromise or settling for less than I deserve. I set the strong intention that there would always be a win-win solution coming out of every situation. Many people argued with me about this point, but I chose to believe it was possible. In my current relationship, we have indeed been able to consistently create those win-win scenarios.

There are no longer any negative aspects on my list about being in a committed relationship. I now have a wonderful partnership where I experience profound support, freedom, respect and joy. However, this could not have occurred until I really observed, addressed and shifted my limiting and negative beliefs about being in a relationship. I could not be where I am if I had not taken responsibility for myself and worked hard to understand and heal myself.

Exercise: Identifying Dueling Intentions

In general, what comes to mind when you think of relationships? Is it joy? Pain? Fun? Betrayal? Happiness? Sadness? More than likely it is a combination of positive and negative qualities. Turn to a blank page in your journal and draw a line down the middle. On one side of the line, list the reasons you want a relationship. On the other side, write down the reasons you do not want to be in a relationship. Look deep within yourself for any dueling intentions or buried beliefs that may need to be identified.

Example:

Reasons I want a relationship	Reasons I do not want a relationship
Companionship	*Compromise/settling*
Mutual support	*Boredom*
Sharing interests	*Feeling trapped*
Having adventures	*Less freedom*
Security	*Potential for pain*
Fidelity	*Monogamy*
Commitment	*Commitment*

Once you are consciously aware of your dueling intentions, you can use this information to clarify what you truly want in a relationship. Review your list of reasons and use them to create your own ideal scenario. This could be done in a form of written prayer that combines the positive characteristics you desire along with constructively addressing your negative concerns.

Example:

I am welcoming and embracing a long-term, loving and committed relationship with a partner who loves his own freedom and supports me wholeheartedly in embracing my own. I am delighted to be experiencing a fulfilling, committed spiritual partnership that is secure with an emotionally available and mature man/woman who appreciates me and our connection. He/she knows how to successfully navigate the more challenging waters of life and we become more intimate with each other as a result of them.

Surrender

There is a significant difference between preference and attachment. We sometimes cannot help that we have preferences and that is fine. However, when we have an attachment, we are more ridged, less flexible and usually setting ourselves up for disappointment. Surrendering is the act of releasing our attachments, softening, relaxing, being patient and no longer relying solely on our own understanding. It is the awareness and acceptance that you are not in complete control of your life. For many, admitting this can be painful and really scary! It means we are willing to loosen our white knuckled grip on life, relinquish our demands, and trust the workings of Spirit and the organizational skills of the universe. It is releasing false illusions so we can invite and experience connection, miracles, joy and truth. It is about living life from the heart rather than the head. It is ultimately about aligning with our Higher Selves and inviting the grace of God into our lives.

Exercise:

1. Use a loose piece of paper and write down any limiting beliefs or fears that you have about being in a committed relationship.

2. Write down any connections or attachments to others that prevent your heart from being truly accessible and available.

3. Are there people from your past that still tug at your heart strings? If so, who?

4. Do you have an attachment to being in relationship with a particular person? If so, who?

5. Is there anyone you have not forgiven or still feel victimized by?

6. Write down other situations, people, challenges, opportunities, relationships or anything else you are now willing to offer up to Spirit.

7. Are you willing to surrender any limiting beliefs and dueling intentions? Are you ready to let go of past relationships you still feel attached to? If your answer is yes, then you are ready to surrender. When you release your attachments and partner with Spirit, you open more fully to intuition, clarity, direction and Divine support. However, this cannot happen without an invitation from you. By surrendering, you are not giving up. You are merely choosing to relax, become receptive, release your worries and have faith in the Source that breathes you.

8. Now create a sacred space for yourself. Perhaps you can light a candle, burn incense and play soothing music. Write the following letter or something similar in your own words:

Dear God/Spirit/ Jesus/ Divine One (or whatever name you choose to use):
I now invite You to partner with me. Please support and assist me on my journey. I am now open to Your plan for me. I am now willing to surrender and release any and all negative, limiting or unhealthy beliefs and attachments. My intention is to be free to love and be love. My intention is to journey forth in partnership with You in great joy, love, clarity and connection. Thank You, Dear God, for all of the blessings in my life and the opportunity to align with You more fully. Thank you for all the love, joy, beauty and blessings in my in my life and all that are on the way to me now!

With love,
(Sign your name)

9. Now tear up or carefully burn the paper you used to answer the questions. By participating in this simple ceremony, you crack the door open for Spirit to show up more fully in your life. The One who created you wants happiness for you, but will not force it upon you. It is up to you to align with Spirit. As best-selling author and spiritual activist Marianne Williamson has said, "The same energy that moves the planets around the sun, that turns seeds into flowers and trees and turns embryos into babies, can take care of your life—if you let Him."

It is by lifting our hands and our hearts to God that we open to greater possibilities, incredible synchronicities, as well as profound healing and love. By doing this we leave behind relying solely on our limited understanding and we open to partnering and flowing with the Creative Energy of the Universe. When the student is ready, the teacher appears. When the lover is ready the beloved appears. If you are truly ready and if your intention is sincere, allow your heart to open and expect miracles.

Chapter 6
The Inner Child

It's never too late to have a happy childhood.
~ Wayne Dyer

In every adult there lurks a child—an eternal child,
something that is always becoming, is never completed, and
calls for unceasing care, attention and education.
That is the part of the human personality which
wants to develop and become whole.
~ Carl Jung

The concept of the Inner Child has been a part of mythology for thousands of years. Fables about the Inner Child are found throughout Roman and Eastern history. Understanding the Inner Child has also been a vital part of modern psychology. Well-known psychologists such as Freud, Alder, Jung and Reich all agreed on the importance of childhood and the Inner Child. Carl Jung referred to the Inner Child as the Divine Child and regarded it as a symbol of wholeness in the psyche.

We all carry within us an eternal child. The Inner Child is the part of us that is alive, energetic, vulnerable, imaginative, creative, courageous, playful and joyful. Cultivating a personal relationship with our Inner Child is vital to personal empowerment. It assists us in becoming conscious and aware of ourselves on a very deep level. It is at the foundation of our beliefs and the most essential aspect of who we are. It is our authentic self.

According to Dr. Charles L. Whitfield, author of *Healing the Child Within*, 80 to 95 percent of people did not receive the love, guidance and nurturing necessary to feel deeply and inherently good about themselves. Even if we were raised in a loving family environment, simply the experience of being born and living in this world creates feelings of abandonment and stress. If our needs for nurturing were not met when we were young, if we did not feel completely accepted and adored, or if we were not allowed sufficient freedom of expression, the Inner Child goes into hiding. We start to adopt behavior that will get us attention or we may put away parts of ourselves so we will be more acceptable to those we love. This is when emotional masks and the "false self" starts to form. These masks may include the jokester, the victim, the people pleaser, the trouble maker and others.

Everyone has difficult experiences from their past. Healing those past hurts is a part of the journey toward personal wholeness. Acknowledging and integrating the Inner Child and bearing witness to the child's pain, grief and disappointments is an essential part of the journey. Although the prospect may seem daunting, strange or unpleasant this work supports us in becoming who we are truly meant to be. It also creates the potential and opportunity to tap into tremendous spiritual power.

While most of us have indeed suffered loss, painful memories and traumatic experiences, our Inner Child, at the deepest level, remains healthy and whole. Whether our childhood experiences were filled with joy or pain, *all of us* can benefit from building a stronger and more conscious relationship with the playful, innocent, essential aspect inside of ourselves. Hence, the healing discussed in this chapter is not really about healing the Inner Child, but rather healing the *painful memories* associated with our youth. The relationship with our Inner Child is strengthened as our pain is remembered, released and healed. This is when our true self can easily and naturally shine forth.

By nature, all children are narcissistic and cannot help but take things personally. When we were young, we believed the world revolved around us because we had not yet learned to reason in any other way. As children, our parents were our "higher power." When they experienced problems or stress, we did not have the conscious ability or objectivity to realize it was not our fault. Irrational beliefs started to form and the foundation of who we are was put into place.

The nature of life tends to be confusing and unpredictable; as a result, most of us experienced a broken heart very early on. Childhood is full of losses—the loss of our sense of oneness with mother; the disillusionment of being all powerful; the loss of magic and fantasy; and the loss of pets, friends, or family. If we are lucky, we have someone who loves us and supports us through our losses. We learn to mourn in a productive, healthy manner and to process pain without being emotionally crippled by it. We learn to process life and create a solid foundation of value. If we do not have this support (or if our parents are not adept at mourning their own losses) we may end up experiencing guilt, anger and shame, then suppress these painful emotions. We may begin to believe we have little value; the world is unsafe; that something is wrong with us or we are not worthy of being loved.

If we did not receive all the love we so deeply longed for as a child, it can haunt us in confusing and complex ways. It can destroy the interpersonal bridge and prevent us from connecting deeply and intimately with others. It also undermines our ability to deal with emotional challenges. If we were wounded as children, we can become "emotionally stunted." If we did not learn to process our grief and mourn our losses, we can get "tangled up" in it. If we did not receive the support and understanding we needed from our parents, they generally become central figures in the drama of our lives. Even if we disconnect from our parents or move far away from them, we will still continue to play out their roles with surrogates. These surrogates usually come in the form of our romantic interests and those to whom we are inexplicably drawn.

The pain from the Inner Child manifests itself in unconscious, immature and often destructive ways. If we are not conscious and cognizant of the Inner Child and the injuries he or she has sustained, we give power over to this young, hurt aspect of ourselves and it rules our lives from the shadows. For example, if we remain unaware of, deny or suppress our pain and disappointments from childhood, we can easily become codependent. People who are codependent look to someone outside of themselves for love and nurturing to soothe their hurts and disillusionments.

If we do not do the work necessary to heal our emotional pain of long ago, anything that has not been resolved will most certainly come up in our intimate relationships. If we truly want to manifest a healthy and satisfying partnership, it is important we become aware of, connect with and heal this aspect of ourselves. We need to revisit the painful memories of our childhood and honor those feelings and experiences. This is the way to release the emotional trauma that tends to control our lives from behind the scenes.

Choosing to remember and release pain from our early childhood takes willingness and courage. I had tremendous resistance to reviewing my childhood until life became unbearably painful and bleak. I finally chose to address my past and invite my Inner Child back into my life in a conscious way.

Extraordinary healing occurs when you go back to the child who still exists inside of you and say, "It wasn't your fault, you didn't do anything wrong. You are a beautiful, wonderful, lovable human being." It is important to acknowledge past hurts and to learn to have compassion for the child that you were (and in many ways still are).

The healing of childhood disillusionment and pain is a process. Experiences at different ages can cause various injuries and affect us in a multitude of ways. Trauma can occur on all levels (physical, mental, emotional and spiritual) and can occur anywhere or with anyone—interactions with our immediate family, friends, strangers, classmates and with members of our church. Experiences that can hurt the Inner Child include:

abuse or witnessing abuse

suppressing emotions

deception

manipulation

threats

criticism

disapproval

being invalidated

being rejected

being abandoned

resentment

blame, or

unrealistic expectations.

Other experiences that negatively influence the way we feel about ourselves are being:

shamed

teased

yelled at

ignored, or

controlled.

Additional experiences that cause significant trauma in childhood are:

loss of family members, pets or friends

moving

changing schools

divorce

remarriage

addictions (alcoholism, drugs, food, etc.)

health problems

fighting

new siblings

harsh discipline

arrests and

natural disasters.

These lists are extensive and may help you realize you have had trauma of which you were not aware. Also, the more sensitive you are, the deeper the painful experiences may affect you.

Sometimes in our healing, integration and growth, we feel like we are taking two steps forward and one step back. This is simply part of the process. You may want to find a therapist who can assist you with the healing process. Growth does not happen in a linear fashion; it occurs in cycles, waves or layers. Healing our memories from childhood can be challenging and confusing. Being gentle with ourselves and giving ourselves more time for solitude can help us integrate our Inner Child, settle within ourselves and become whole.

Healing the layers of childhood memories can be a life-long process. I did a great deal of work to heal my Inner Child before connecting with my husband, Steve. This was important and necessary to help me get ready to meet him.

How Old Are You Now?

Steve and I constantly assist one another in fine tuning our inner relationships and understanding our Inner Children. When one of us is highly emotional, the other will ask, "How old are you now?" Whether we are experiencing joy, pain or sadness, it is always interesting to pose this question and listen to the response. The response is usually subconscious and accurate.

One day, Steve was playing video games with his son. He looked very happy, engrossed and entertained. When I asked him how old he was, he laughed and said, "I'm 15!" Another time I was looking forward to going out to see a movie and Steve was not up for it. I was very disappointed. He asked me how old I was. I pouted and said "I'm 6!"

Although we may reside in grown up bodies, we still carry around the hurt and disappointments from our distant past. When we are aware of our subconscious or internal age when we are hurting, it gives us the tools and the ability to communicate and, if necessary, soothe our Inner Child. Anytime we experience anything painful, there is usually a thread of this emotion connecting us to our past. We are rarely dealing with just the matter at hand; we are dealing with the lineage of our personal human experience. When I am with clients that are in emotional distress, I ask them if they can recall an experience from their past that feels like the current hurt or challenge. The memory usually dates back to an early time in childhood. By becoming conscious of the pain in our past, we can comfort the Inner Child who is suffering and help alleviate our present pain. When we have this awareness and ability to soothe ourselves, we unravel the pain from the bottom up. We no longer have to unconsciously recreate the same scenario and suffering over and over again.

Tim and Shonda

I recently met with a couple I will call Tim and Shonda. They often found themselves in conflict; both of them going to their corner, defending their positions, trying to get their needs met and verbally "duking it out." A frequent point of contention was Tim's desire to hang out with his guy friends and play golf on the weekends. Shonda's vision of their weekends included the two of them traveling, communicating and connecting. She often ended up feeling angry, hurt and abandoned by his choices. When we addressed this issue, I asked Shonda to tell me the first time she remembered having this sort of emotional experience. She thought about it for awhile and then tears started to well up in her eyes. She said when she was in second grade, she wanted to spend time with her father on the weekends, but he had no desire to do so. She witnessed her mother trying to convince him to spend time with her.

Shonda's father would yell angrily saying he worked hard all week and did not want to have to babysit Shonda during his time off. Shonda felt ashamed, unloved, abandoned and very, very sad—a significant childhood wound.

I also worked with Tim and asked him about his emotional experiences regarding golfing and spending time with his friends on the weekends. I asked him what it brought up for him when Shonda tried to talk him out of going. He told me he felt rebellious, frustrated and angry. It brought back memories of his mother wanting him to babysit his little brother, rather than allowing him to spend time with his friends and doing the things that he wanted to do. This was one of Tim's original childhood wounds.

They both had difficult experiences as children; they both felt dishonored, unimportant, frustrated, angry and sad. These experiences were now playing out in their adult lives. When I got them together and asked Shonda how old this hurt part of her was, she said she experienced it at age 7. When I asked Tim how old this frustrated, angry part of him was, he said it was from age 10. In this situation, we were not simply dealing with two adults and the issue of "to golf or not to golf." There was a sad 7-year-old girl that was looking to Tim to make her feel loved and important, like her father had not. There was also an angry 10-year-old boy that was rebelling against his mother and did not want to be told what to do.

Neither Tim nor Shonda were aware of all the dynamics going on in this situation or how to deal with them—they just knew they felt awful. As they listened to each other, they became aware of how deep the issues ran for one another. They started to see the situation from a higher altitude and with more compassion for each other—and for themselves. As Shonda spoke about her sadness from childhood, Tim empathized with her. He started to understand the depth of her feelings and offered to spend the upcoming weekend together doing things they both enjoyed. He also started to realize that Shonda was not his mother telling him what he could and could not do.

Shonda also empathized with Tim's situation (having a younger sister herself) and said she would support Tim in golfing with his friends once or twice a month. Shonda was willing to take more responsibility for herself by entertaining her own Inner Child. She would spend time with her friends, create artwork or go to a movie that her Inner Child chooses. Tim and Shonda's challenge was easily resolved once the couple became aware of their difficult childhood experiences and early disappointments.

The next time you have an emotional experience—positive or negative—stop and ask yourself, "How old am I now?" You may be surprised by the age that comes forth. By becoming aware of and implementing this simple exercise, you can take better care of yourself and experience greater understanding. You will also be better equipped to communicate and move beyond uncomfortable emotions. You might also be highly entertained by your own silliness and joy!

If we do not take responsibility for our painful childhood memories, we will seek out someone else to fix our pain. We set ourselves up for continued disillusionment, pain and betrayal. In order to heal and relax into our wholeness, it is ultimately up to each individual to become aware of, care for and to soothe the parts of themselves that have been neglected, disappointed or hurt.

Once you accept and integrate your Inner Child, you are more able to be who you truly are. Rather than hiding behind emotional masks for fear of rejection, you can bring forth all of yourself into a relationship. You will no longer hesitate to express your true thoughts or feelings, because you will no longer depend on someone else for the experience of fulfillment or wholeness. When you love and approve of yourself, love and approval from someone else is no longer a primary motivating force in your life.

When you understand, adore and care for your Inner Child, it decreases the burden, demands or expectations that you unknowingly and unwittingly place on another person. It also increases opportunities for honest and supportive communication. This is the environment in which a mature relationship and authentic spiritual partnership can naturally flourish.

Exercise: Embracing Your Inner Child

1. Set aside an hour. Create an environment where you will not be disturbed and where you will feel safe. You may want to light a candle, burn incense or play soft music. You may even want to find a picture of yourself as a child.

2. Set an intention for healing, clarity and integration.

3. Have your journal handy along with some pens, pencils or even crayons.

4. Say a prayer or an invocation and invite your Inner Child to come forward to communicate with you. Make sure to let him or her know that you really want to connect. During this exercise, resist judging yourself as wrong, bad or silly. Accept whatever you are feeling or experiencing as valid. What is most essential is to connect with your Inner Child in a genuine, safe and loving way and to bring your current love and compassion to this younger part of you.

5. With your dominant hand, write what you would like to say to your Inner Child. Perhaps request they join you for a heart-to-heart conversation.

6. Using your other hand, allow your Inner Child to respond to you in writing. You may choose to use a different writing utensil or a crayon. (Let your Inner Child choose the color they want to use.) Do not worry if your writing is awkward or illegible. You simply need to understand what the Inner Child is attempting to communicate.

7. After your Inner Child has expressed themself, let the adult part of you respond (again with your dominant hand). Do your best to be compassionate, understanding, loving and kind.

8. Allow your Inner Child to respond to you, again writing with your other hand.

9. Allow this exchange to occur for as long as needed. You may find that your Inner Child is very hurt and has a lot to say. They might be resistant to opening up to you; perhaps they are sad or angry for being ignored for so long. Just allow whatever emotions are present to come forth in this safe and sacred environment. The Inner Child wants only for your happiness and is always on your side. However, he or she may not believe that you are on *their* side. Be sure to let them know you are indeed on their side and want them to be happy, heard, safe and fulfilled.

10. Near the end of the process, ask your Inner Child if he or she wants or needs anything from you at this time. Perhaps there is an activity they want to experience or a teddy bear or toy they want to buy. Let them know you care about what they think and how they feel. Be sure to follow through with any commitments you make.

11. When you feel complete, let your Inner Child know you want to maintain the relationship and express your appreciation.

12. Take a few moments to acknowledge yourself for your willingness to open the door to this younger essential part of you. This is a powerful and profound step in becoming "whole unto yourself." Again, the key component in this exercise is to bring the powerful healing presence of your own love into the relationship.

When we open the door to our Inner Child and invite them back into our lives in a conscious and deliberate way, we become aware of our deep feelings and beliefs. We also have the capacity and ability to bring compassion, kindness, light and love to the places inside that hurt. These are the qualities that are at the very heart of all healing. This shifts us in positive and powerful ways. As we shift and heal, we transform, integrate and become whole.

By remembering and then releasing stored, dormant or unconscious pain, we open up. This creates the space for more love inside of ourselves. There is less chaos in our psyche, therefore less chaos in our relationships and lives. We feel more relaxed and comfortable in our skin. We become more intuitive, centered, authentic and peaceful. When this happens, the natural by-product is that we accept, approve and care for ourselves in deeper and more powerful ways.

We should make ourselves available for dialogue with the Inner Child at all times. Our Inner Child should be our friend and an aspect we are very aware of, respect, protect and adore. The natural progression of healing the painful memories of our Inner Child is getting back to the place of the "True Inner Child," the true essence of who we are which is laughter, creativity, connection, happiness and love.

As you continue the process of writing in your journal, you may get to the point where you want to ask your Inner Child: What are some of your favorite memories? What makes you happy? What it is you really want to do? What colors do you like? What do you like to wear? This can be a very interesting and enjoyable part of the healing process. I was surprised that my Inner Child wanted to pick flowers, wear more purple, paint, go to the library and eat Mexican food. These are experiences and activities my adult self would never have considered! Once I become aware of this part of me, I was better able to fulfill my own needs and desires. I was no longer walking around in unconscious deficit, hoping to meet someone who could make me feel better.

When we recognize and embrace our Inner Child, we laugh more, play more and experience greater happiness. Setting boundaries is done with more clarity and ease. The thing that is so powerful about understanding our Inner Child is that it changes the core relationship we have with ourselves. Once we have this more loving relationship with ourselves, all of our relationships change and life naturally improves. We understand our value and can easily speak our truth. We are also authentically empowered, more fully present and capable of the most remarkable joy!

Chapter 7
Forgiveness

To forgive is to set a prisoner free and
discover the prisoner was you.
~ Lewis B. Smedes

When you forgive, you in no way change the past—
but you sure do change the future.
~ Bernard Meltzer

One of the most important things we can do to make ourselves available for a loving relationship is to forgive. When we feel someone has wronged us or we have been victimized, we maintain a negative bond to that very person. By choosing to withhold forgiveness, not only do we only lower our vibration, we also create a dynamic where we will inevitably be victimized again. By choosing to forgive, we raise our vibration and sever the connection we have to those we are holding in judgment in our minds and in our lives. We must invite forgiveness if we want to liberate ourselves, reclaim our power and become available for true heart connections.

Forgiveness can be difficult for many reasons. Perhaps you have been abused, taken advantage of, stolen from, lied to, hurt or disrespected. Maybe you have been abandoned, betrayed, or disregarded. It is hard to forgive someone who has been thoughtless or mean and even harder if someone has been deliberate or malicious in their intentions. And really, *why should we forgive?* Ultimately, we forgive so that our hearts are available to ourselves and to others; we forgive so we may be free.

Releasing Negative Thought Forms

At the heart of forgiveness is the recognition that what we are letting go of are negative thought forms. We greatly benefit from identifying and releasing the judgments and thoughts that darken our inner terrain and keep us energetically linked to those we choose not to forgive. When we choose not to forgive, we carry a "right vs. wrong" orientation inside of ourselves. We place a judgment or negative damnation on another human being and sometimes even ourselves. Whenever any type of judgment is inserted into our consciousness, we carry it in our hearts and we ultimately pay the price. We essentially become a prisoner of our own making. To free ourselves from this destructive energy, it is absolutely essential to identify the people we have not forgiven and the judgments we hold against them.

Forgiveness does not mean we let someone off the hook, or even suggest what they did was acceptable. We do not have to like the person we are forgiving or allow them back into our lives. By forgiving, we sever the cords that bind us to our "perpetrator." We forgive so we do not have to repeat the storyline or the circumstances. We forgive so we can fully own our power. We forgive so we can experience life from the natural state of joy and love.

My Story of Forgiveness

My personal story of forgiveness was an extraordinary healing experience and instrumental in my evolution. Through the process of forgiveness, I reclaimed my authentic power, discovered my life's purpose and manifested true love.

I was in a relationship with Bob for three years. It started out as instant attraction, a compelling connection and a wonderful adventure. We planned to get married, so I gave up my career for him and I did my best to support him mentally, emotionally and physically. My therapist told me this was "my job" and my priest said this was "the way it should be." They were more educated than me and I was certain they were more intelligent, so I thought they must be right.

Eventually, it became apparent the man I was engaged to had some deep-seated angst and struggled with addictions. However, I firmly held onto the notion that I could make things better; he had such extraordinary potential and I really believed I could "fix" him.

After two years, our relationship went into serious decline. Life was no longer fun; in fact, it was confusing and very painful. At one point, I caught him with another woman. I was devastated. I thought about leaving, but decided I wanted to work things out and stayed in the relationship. I prayed constantly for assistance. I was incredibly depressed and tried many different types of anti-depressants, none of which my body could tolerate. The therapist yelled at me and insisted that I was "resisting treatment." It was not my intention to resist treatment, I wanted to be cooperative and do the right thing. I was doing my very best to hold Bob (and myself) together, but it was not working. I changed my prayer from "God, help me make this work" to "God, if I need to surrender this relationship for me to know myself and for me to know You, I give up. I cannot keep living this way."

Shortly afterwards, Bob and I were scheduled to meet for a couples counseling session. He did not show up. The therapist told me that Bob had a new life and would not be coming back. I did not understand, *we were supposed to get married!* I asked her questions which she refused to answer. I did not have an income (he took care of my bills) and my things were still at his house. What was I supposed to do? My head was spinning and I felt like throwing up. The therapist suggested that I contact an attorney. I left her office dizzy and bewildered.

Some of my questions were answered that night while I was watching television. Bob was being interviewed and he told the reporter (and the world) that he had found a new love. I was stunned. I called the therapist, my priest, my friends and Bob—no one would speak to me. I felt my life was over and could not think of any reason to go on. I was sick with a multitude of health problems and I felt exhausted. I had no money, no job, no friends and no direction. I felt as if I had no value, no purpose and no life. I was a "no-thing."

This was my "dark night of the soul." Life was incredibly bleak; I felt completely abandoned, ugly, stupid, betrayed, terrified and alone. I fantasized about suicide. I had a heart-to-heart conversation with God and told Him I was scared and wanted to come home. Incredibly, I felt I was being comforted and understood that everything was going to be okay. Right now, all I had to do was to keep breathing and putting one foot in front of the other.

I lit a candle in my bedroom and looked in the mirror through my tears. My face looked so haggard and forlorn—I hardly recognized myself. What had happened to me? What had become of my life? As I continued looking at myself, the face seemed to change; it seemed there were all these different people looking at me. There was so much pain in their eyes. Then a thought came to me. If I had the courage to live, perhaps one day I could light the way for others who are hurting. What happened to me might be bigger than my small story. Perhaps I was crazy or delusional, but the thought gave me hope. I told God if I could figure out a way to pay my bills, I would hold onto life. I asked for direction and guidance. As I wandered around in state of shock the next day, a neighbor told me about a school that taught massage, polarity balancing and focused on the mind-body-spirit connection. I thought it might provide a way for me to make money and also support my healing process, so I decided to check out the school.

The school felt "right" and was good for me on many levels. However, my ego did not like it very much. I had been used to limousines, red carpets, private jets and personal shoppers. Now I was schlepping around a massage table for very little money. In retrospect, the school was exactly what I needed. It also introduced me to the concept of forgiveness. I thought to myself, "No way!" I would *never* be able to forgive Bob, the therapist or my priest." Honestly, I did not even want to try. I was the victim of a stingy, selfish, narcissistic man and his posse. He treated me horribly; he left me broke and broken. He was the big, mean, powerful monster and I was the innocent bunny rabbit he had squashed.

Two years later, life was still challenging and painful and I could not figure out why. I still felt like a victim in every area of life—family, business, friendships and romance. I could not seem to move forward. When I meditated about this, the message I received was: "You cannot move forward when you are constantly turning around and looking at your past." I was facing the wrong direction!

Then someone told me a story about a veteran who had been a prisoner of war in Vietnam. He suffered some horrible experiences and barely survived. He met another man who had also been a P.O.W. The first man asked him if he had forgiven his captors yet. The second veteran said, "No, and I don't think I ever will." The first man replied, "Oh, so you are still in prison." I was starting to get it, I was miserable because I was still in prison and forgiveness was the key to my freedom.

I also considered the question, "Do you want to be right or do you want to be happy?" I really wanted both, but I was realizing perhaps that was going to be impossible. I was going to have to open my mind to forgiveness, but how? How do I forgive someone who was so horrible to me?

It all started with intention. My intention was to open my mind to the *possibility* that I could forgive Bob and the others who had "victimized" me. The second step was to allow myself to feel my feelings. I had gone from hurt and victimhood straight to depression and then stayed there. I never allowed myself to feel my anger. I decided it was time.

Anger can be a powerful tool in the healing process. Safely expressing anger can move energy and give life to someone trapped in the swampy experience of depression and despair. Elisabeth Kübler-Ross, one of the world's foremost authority on healing grief, had been known to say, "We finish our own unfinished business." She taught a technique in which a rubber hose is used to beat a pillow for the purpose of releasing anger. I did not have a rubber hose, but I did have an old tennis racket. I decided I would give it a try.

I was really ready to let go of all the anger that had been repressed for so long. I fluffed up my pillows, invited Spirit in and set the intention to heal and release whatever was no longer serving me. At first, smacking the pillow with the tennis racket seemed a little silly. However, as I continued, I felt genuine emotion start to bubble up. I allowed the experience to be what it was and the anger continued to build. I grabbed another pillow and started screaming into it while beating the other one senseless. As I allowed the expression of my anger, I started to articulate thoughts, feelings and questions. The experience led me to a question that had been buried in my subconscious for a very long time. I repeated it over and over: *"What about me? What about me?"*

I yelled and screamed until all of the charge was gone. I was spent. I ended up on the floor crying again, but this time it was different. The question was not just for Bob, it was for my dad, for God and for me. I felt forgotten by everyone, including myself. It had been a long time since I had been my own priority. Bob was not the first man to abandon and betray me. I had a long history of this, starting with my father who I doubted ever really loved me. This was my original source of abandonment and it seemed I was recreating this experience over and over again. I had suppressed and ignored the pain. It was in the distant past and I thought I had moved on with my life. However, it was not forgotten in my subconscious mind. On a very deep level, I believed I was inherently "not enough" and life continued to mirror this restricted, suppressed belief back to me.

I began to understand the relationships I had manifested were simply reflections of my deeply held thoughts and beliefs. My failed relationship with Bob presented me with the opportunity to get in touch with my original pain and to evaluate what I held to be true. We all attract people into our lives that lead us to relive our original painful experiences. Most of us go through the motions many times before we notice a pattern. When my beliefs were finally exposed making my pattern absolutely clear, I then had the opportunity to make more conscious choices and open up to different possibilities. My healing was now well underway.

In order to heal and transform the energy of anything, we need to experience it deeply and then let it go. As we make the choice to heal our trauma and pain, we have the opportunity to become the wounded healer. Every human being is given the opportunity to heal their wounds and then light the way for others who are a few steps behind them. I knew I wanted to help others, I just resisted letting go of my story.

I was starting to see my situation from a higher perspective; I was getting the bigger picture. My heart and mind were finally opening and I was beginning to feel myself shift. Most of us are not taught to look around and say, "Look at the mess I have created." Instead, we are taught to judge, blame, accuse, seek revenge and be the victim. We remain trapped when we continue to identify ourselves as the victim. We vibrate at such a frequency that we inevitably attract another "perpetrator"—like the north and south poles of two magnets, we will find one another.

Soul Lessons

When we are willing to let go of our victim identity, our small stories and our negativity, we start to gain altitude. We can begin to observe our lives from a higher perspective. The choice to perceive any situation with a spiritual context can lift us up and help us to see things with greater clarity.

Where we place our focus and faith is crucial. We can choose to put our faith in the human world of limitations or we can choose to put our faith in a universe of limitless good. We all put our faith somewhere, whether we are consciously aware of it or not. Where we choose to place our faith will ultimately determine the themes and experiences of our lives.

A Course in Miracles, a wonderful spiritual and psychological self-study program that focuses on forgiveness of self and others tells us, "God has sent you nothing but angels." Everyone who comes into our lives, (even, and maybe especially, the "perpetrators") has the potential to be a healing angel. Healing can begin the instant we are willing to consider that our soul, or Higher Self, lovingly created the challenging situations for our highest good; for the purpose of learning and taking greater personal responsibility. Seemingly terrible situations occur as an opportunity or a key to our growth. These opportunities are presented so we may become aware of what has prevented us from being as happy as we can be. When we understand this, we can finally embark upon the path of becoming whole, aligned and conscious. Whether we realize it or not, life is a spiritual journey and our most profound and significant teachers may be the people that have caused us the most pain and grief in our lives.

When I thought about my relationship with Bob and all the people who hurt me, I finally arrived at the place where I wanted to understand what caused this to happen. I wanted to see the bigger picture. I asked myself, "What is my soul trying to learn? What are my lessons?" The answer that came forward was I needed to believe in myself. I needed to trust my power, my intuition and my heart. I realized I needed to start making myself more of a priority, tighten up my boundaries and become more discerning. These were significant life lessons that have changed me in positive and profound ways.

Three Questions

If there are people in your life you have not forgiven, take a moment to answer these three questions.

What are the lessons my soul is trying to learn?
What are the blessings?
What am I grateful for?

When we answer these three questions, we gain "altitude." We can begin to see our relationships and challenges from a higher perspective. It can give us a glimpse of the bigger picture, from the perspective of a soaring eagle rather than a frightened mouse. When we consciously choose to forgive the people that have caused us pain, we remove roadblocks and loosen constrictions within ourselves. This frees our energy so it is available for creativity, healing and true love. By choosing to deeply and authentically forgive, we open the door to our own freedom. We increase our vibration and move in the direction of our power, passion and purpose.

When we feel discomfort, it is a signal that something is out of alignment. It presents an opportunity for us to become aware of the situation and heal ourselves. It could be a toxic belief or a false core belief that keeps us from being our truest self. If we judge, blame and play the victim, we are missing the opportunity to heal. Inevitably, our souls will assist us in creating more pain, until we are forced to ask, "What is going on?" For some people, the message has to be very loud and quite extreme before they choose to pay attention. Some will even die before they get the message.

We cannot force the process of forgiveness. When we are in immense pain, it is virtually impossible to get there. In the aftermath of a disaster or in the heat of anger, we need to process our emotions—we need to feel our feelings.

However, even in those challenging moments, we can set an intention to eventually forgive by asking Spirit to help us release and forgive those who have hurt us. In other words, we can open our hearts to the possibility of forgiveness in the future by asking God to allow His loving presence and the energy of His forgiveness to flow through us. I do not know of anyone who has uttered this powerful, prayerful request for His help and been ignored or denied.

Creating Closure

I felt that my anger needed a physical outlet before I would be able to create closure and authentically forgive those who hurt me. Yelling and hitting pillows with a tennis racket helped me to move the suppressed energy. Writing letters was also immensely helpful. I wrote a series of letters to Bob, the therapist and my priest. I did not mail any of them; I wrote the letters solely for the purpose of releasing emotions and to bring about my own personal healing. I realized none of these people would provide the closure I needed, so I was going to have to create it for myself.

The first letters were full of anger and hurt. I said everything I wanted to say to these people. Over time, the energy and emotion of the letters started to change. A few of them were very sad. I felt as if my Inner Child needed to express her pain and confusion about being abandoned. As I went through the process, I also felt compelled to write a letter to my father and to God. I felt significant changes starting to occur—each letter created a shift within myself. The pain and sadness came out of me in layers. As I gave a voice and an outlet to all that I had suppressed, I was starting to feel a ray of light piercing through the confusion and darkness. I was experiencing more hope, peace and optimism. Things were coming into focus; the healing experience of authentic forgiveness was taking place.

Creating artwork was another outlet for my anger and sadness that helped me tremendously. You do not need to be an artist for this to be a powerful part of the healing process. There were times I simply pulled out big pieces of paper, canvases, crayons, charcoals or paint. I used whatever color and medium I was drawn to at the moment. I often made a mess, but it gave me enormous relief. Creating art is potentially a significant and valuable tool for healing.

Exercise: Forgiveness Visualization

This exercise will help you sever your connections to those who have hurt you. You may read through each step and do the exercise by memory, have someone read the exercise aloud to you or listen to a recording of it in your own voice. Go slowly and give yourself the opportunity to really visualize and *feel* your emotions. It may take more than once to fully disconnect, but you should feel some relief each time you do this exercise.

1. Relax, close your eyes and take a few deep, cleansing breaths. Now allow the person who you would benefit the most from forgiving right now to easily come into your mind's eye.

2. Visualize this person standing about 10 feet away from you and with a cord connecting the two of you.

3. Invite your guardian angel, your Higher Self, or God to join you. This Being has your greatest interest at heart and is here to protect, love and support you through this process.

4 Take your time and express what you are thinking and how you are feeling to this person who has hurt you. Tell them everything that is on your mind and in your heart.

5. When you are finished, you may find that the person would like to say something to you. Allow them to express themselves. You may want to respond and let the dialogue continue.

6. When the dialogue is complete, you may want to ask your Higher Self or guardian angel what your soul has

been trying to learn from this relationship. They may be able to show or tell you about the higher purpose of this challenging relationship or experience.

7. When your Higher Self or angel is done sharing the message with you and you feel you are ready to release the person who has hurt you, notice that your Higher Self or angel has a pair of golden scissors. You may ask them to assist you in severing the connection with this person. Tell them you are now ready to release the cords that bind you. Tell them you are ready to accept your highest calling and claim your life's destiny. Proclaim you are ready to be free.

8. Sever the cord.

9. After the cord has been cut, imagine surrounding yourself with a circle of light or a protective iridescent bubble. You are now establishing new boundaries and are no longer a victim of this person. If you think of or see this person, you will feel safe and whole unto yourself. Bless them on their path and know you are now free, supported and blessed on yours.

After completing this forgiveness visualization you may want to write your thoughts, feelings or revelations in your journal. Express gratitude to Spirit for the healing that is occurring on all levels and for the wonderful opportunities and relationships that are on their way to you now!

Exercise: Freedom through Self-Forgiveness

The last crucial part of my forgiveness process was forgiving myself. Beneath all the judgments I held against the other people who had wronged me, were the judgments I held against myself. I judged myself as stupid, naive, ugly, inept, fat, unworthy, lazy, unlovable and a mistake. When we identify and release the judgments we hold against ourselves, we heal our core relationship with our Self. This subsequently supports us in shifting and healing our perceptions and our relationships.

1. Open your journal and write about a recent situation where you felt someone wronged you.

   Example: *My fiancé had our therapist tell me the relationship was over and he never wanted to see me again. I felt devastated, confused, grief stricken and deep pain.*

2. Take a few minutes to review what you just wrote and see if you can identify any negative judgments you have placed on the other person. One key is to look for any "right vs. wrong" thinking (that is, what should have happened?).

   Example: *Bob is a cruel, insensitive man. He should have communicated with me personally. He should have had the guts, respect and the integrity to talk to me, but he did not. I am right and he is wrong.*

3. Write down any underlying negative thoughts you have been holding against yourself.

   Example: *I am stupid, naïve and an idiot for staying so long in this terrible relationship. Maybe I was a bad girlfriend and didn't even deserve to be loved.*

4. Once you have identified negative judgments about yourself, create your self- forgiveness statements.

Example: *I forgive myself for telling myself that I am stupid, I forgive myself for believing that I am naive, I forgive myself for calling myself an idiot. I forgive myself for judging myself as not worthy of being loved.*

5. When you are ready to release these judgments, allow yourself to bring your awareness to your heart, perhaps you want to place your hand over it, let your energy settle there and say your forgiveness statements out loud.

   Example: *I forgive myself for judging myself as stupid. I forgive myself for judging myself as an idiot. I forgive myself for judging myself as unworthy of love.*

6. Finally, what truth statements might you bring forward that are a more accurate expression of the bigger picture about this other person, yourself and this situation? Write them down and then say them out loud.

   Example of a truth statement about the other person: *The truth about this man is that he is deeply wounded, has experienced great pain and has many fears. He was terrified to talk to me directly about his feelings and decision— none of which has anything to do with me nor is it a reflection of my value.*

   Example of a truth statement about me: *Although I am human and have made mistakes, I know I am a good person and am doing my very best. I am God's child and I deserve to be loved and adored. I am the child in whom God is well pleased.*

   Example of a truth statement of this situation: *I know everything that is happening in my life is supporting me in my growth, healing and expansion in consciousness. The truth is I know that God is on my side. I know I am being supported in becoming stronger and becoming the very best me I can be.*

When we complete our forgiveness and truth statements, it gives us the opportunity to reframe our human experience and to see ourselves from a more accurate perspective. When we are willing to take the time to see ourselves from this higher perspective, a power is unleashed and we align with our Higher Self and Spirit. Forgiveness opens our hearts and paves the way for miracles.

Forgiveness is an attitude and choice of compassion for oneself and others. Through forgiveness we can transform our suffering into self-knowledge and spiritual growth. With forgiveness, we release our ego's need to be right and its incessant need to judge everyone and everything. It takes awareness, courage and commitment. Now when I feel discomfort, I ask myself what or who am I judging. Once identified, I immediately practice forgiveness and self-forgiveness.

The last letter I wrote to Bob was one of gratitude. He ended up being one of the most significant healing angels in my life. I experienced many blessings by virtue of my earthly dance with him—the way he came into my life, our experiences together and the way we parted. If Bob had stayed in my life, I realize I never would have taken full responsibility for myself. I lived in his shadow and I know I would have stayed there. I never would have picked up a paint brush, never would have gone to school and never would have written a book. He was an actor in the drama of my life and the perfect catalyst for my healing. Because of my experiences with him, I was able to arrive at the place where I could look at myself honestly and deeply. I identified and released a lifetime of powerful judgments I had placed against God, myself my parents and others. I became aware of and transformed my negative, unconscious feelings and beliefs. I was then ready and able to claim my true Self. From this new place of clarity, I am authentic, congruent, peaceful, joyful, healthy and whole. The incredible healing power of forgiveness lifted me up to a place of altitude and gratitude. It also opened up the space in my heart to bring forth the love of my life and assisted me in creating the life of my dreams.

Chapter 8
Guilt and Shame

Shame is the lie someone told you about yourself.
~ Anais Nin

Guilt is the source of sorrows, the avenging fiend that follows us behind with whips and stings.
~ Nicholas Rowe

The qualities of guilt and shame are seemingly inherent in the human experience and the area where some of the deepest judgments and pain reside. Most individuals on a healing path will eventually come face to face with these challenging emotions. In fact, I believe many people avoid embarking on the path of self-awareness for fear of confronting them. Having the experience of personal guilt and shame can range from a minor sense of inferiority and inadequacy to debilitating and profound self-loathing.

Although guilt and shame can be similar in nature, there are some differences. Guilt is what we experience when we believe we have done something wrong or bad. Shame occurs when we believes there is something intrinsically offensive, wrong, bad or flawed within ourselves. Guilt is what we do; shame is who we are.

Well-meaning parents or teachers may have shamed us in order to get us to behave or to establish boundaries. Shame is often used to keep young people clothed and appropriate in the world, thus creating issues around sexuality and the body. A child that grows up in a guilt or shame-based environment will take on this negative energy and it will likely become part of their identity.

People who carry the burden of guilt or shame wear a false mask in order to hide or convince others they are actually okay. They have a deep fear of being exposed. If a person carries significant shame, his or her relationships will not be based on a foundation of truth. Games, manipulation and drama will be powerful forces in their lives. The life of a shame-based individual is about avoidance, secrecy, darkness, deception, fear and denial.

The experience of toxic shame is a sense of feeling innately defective, unworthy or inferior. Toxic shame is often at the core of neurosis, addictions, character disorders and violence. This is a destructive force in humanity and can be a primary contributing factor in the contemplation, attempt or success of suicide.

Guilt keeps a person in a pattern of self-deprecation and non-acceptance, making it impossible to experience true intimacy. It is difficult, if not impossible, to have authentic connections if we have not addressed and healed our personal guilt or shame. In order to reveal ourselves honestly, we must believe the essence of who we are is not only acceptable, but a wonderful gift we want to share.

People who harbor toxic levels of guilt or shame may struggle with these experiences:

Discomfort with emotions or an inability to allow feelings

A sense of loneliness, emptiness or not quite "fitting in"

A deep sense of unworthiness or lack of personal value

Difficulty in expressing their truth

Difficulty with self-assertion

Distorted self image or inconsistent perception of self (feeling superior and/or inferior)

Highly judgmental of self or others

Compulsive or addictive behavior

Constant self-justification

Perfectionism

Overly materialistic

Rigid in behavior or thinking

Denies or dwells on mistakes

Painfully shy or self-conscious

Anxiety and/or depression

Feeling or often stating they do not want to be a burden

Identity, value, or esteem derived from outside themselves (relationships, money, work accomplishments, material objects)

Tells fibs, white lies, untruths or is a compulsive liar

Has a fear of "being in trouble"

If someone suffers from intense shame, it is generally because it has been handed down from parents or caretakers. It is impossible to instill self-love or self-esteem in a child if the caregiver does not authentically value or love themselves. We cannot teach what we do not know.

As infants, we are completely helpless and look to our primary caretakers to supply all of our needs. We determine who we are from the mirroring eyes of our parents. Ideally, when we are babies, our mothers mirror back to us our behavior—when we coo, she coos; when we laugh, she laughs. She takes care of our needs—when we are hungry mother feeds us; when our diapers are wet, mother changes them. However, if our primary caretaker is out of sync with our rhythm and we do not get what we need when we need it, confusion and shame begins to occur. This is when the interpersonal bridge starts to deteriorate and a gap is introduced between us and this important other. This can start to create an emptiness or hole in our soul, which will likely be the catalyst for addictive behavior later on. As adults, when we feel empty we may try to "fill up" with alcohol, drugs, sex, pornography, food, work or relationships.

If a parent was not well cared for as a child, they are most likely wounded and emotionally stunted themselves. They may then actually look to their children to unconsciously fulfill *their* unmet needs and desires. When parents make themselves the priority, the child's needs are rarely met and the negative cycle of shame continues. Children in the contaminated environment of shame often grow up without the experience of unconditional love. They grow up and become "adult children." No matter how much they consume from the outside world, wounded adult children can never get enough to make themselves feel valued, fulfilled and worthy. This hole in the soul cannot be healed by anything other than a healthy relationship with oneself.

Julie's Story

Julie had a history of addiction and destructive behavior. Her pain finally brought Julie to the place of looking within and embarking on her healing path. She began to contemplate her childhood and the initiation of her core beliefs. She had always been painfully shy and seemed to carry a great deal of shame. One night Julie had a vivid dream. In her dream, Julie was sitting on a couch, when she looked down and noticed a cherry pie. Upon closer inspection, Julie saw that this pie was rotten and filled with maggots. She was horrified and ashamed. She then remembered that there was an older pie behind the couch. Julie was mortified at the prospect of how bad that pie would be since it had been there much longer. With trepidation, she looked behind the couch and was amazed to see the freshest, most beautiful perfect cherry pie she had ever seen. Julie felt confused, relieved and happy all at the same time.

She asked me what I thought the dream might mean. Julie was starting to look within and was beginning to encounter her "worms, bats and stinky stuff," as symbolized by her contaminated cherry pie. She had been struggling with a belief that she was inherently rotten. Her dream was communicating that, although things were uncomfortable now, if she continued on her healing path and was willing to look deeper, she would discover that ultimately she is fresh, beautiful, perfect and amazing. Julie cried as she began to understand the deep and profound message of this dream.

Julie continues to look within and take responsibility for her healing. She is allowing the experience of her feelings and is communicating more authentically. Julie has reframed her belief systems and has now come to understand that her true essence is glorious! By choosing to confront her shame-based issues, she is working through them. She is no longer participating in her destructive, addictive behaviors and she is happier, healthier and more beautiful than ever.

Many of us are afraid to look within for the same reason. One of the greatest human fears is that we are unlovable or inadequate. Unworthiness is a challenge almost everyone struggles with either consciously or unconsciously. As we become aware of our feelings of unworthiness, we begin to have some power over it. If we follow through with the healing of our shame-based issues, we eventually arrive at the place of self-acceptance. When we liberate ourselves from the burden of guilt and shame, we then have the opportunity to experience love, joy and acceptance and we will soar.

While processing and releasing guilt and shame, it is important to be gentle and kind with ourselves. We must be introspective and honest. If we feel responsible for a regrettable action, it is beneficial to admit our mistake, learn from it, apologize and set the intention not to repeat it. Most importantly, we must forgive and have compassion for ourselves.

Making mistakes is a part of the human experience. If you do not make mistakes, not only are you not normal—you probably would not be here! The ability to "allow your flaws" and to forgive yourself is vital in establishing a healthy self-esteem and having a joyful life experience.

If we do not confront and heal our guilt and shame, it will continue to be a part of our inner reality and our vibration. It will continue to be reflected in our lives. If we have guilt and shame about eating chocolate cake, we will not drop the weight. When we drop our judgment and our shame, we can more easily drop the weight. If we believe we are a mistake or unworthy of love, our vibration will attract situations and relationships that reflect and reinforce our feelings of inadequacy.

Learning to accept and be compassionate with yourself is vital in the healing process. By choosing to be kind and loving to yourself, you have the opportunity to re-parent and retrain yourself.

Exercise: Releasing Guilt and Shame

Write the answers to these questions in your journal.

1. Identify something for which you feel guilty and ashamed. Remember, guilt is what we do and shame is who we are.

    Example of guilt:
    I feel guilty about the chocolate cake I ate today.

    Example of shame:
    I am a fat, ugly pig. (There is often a shame-based belief beneath the guilt.)

    Example of the deeper shame-based belief:
    I take up too much space.

2. Identify the underlying negative thoughts and judgments you are holding against yourself.

    Example of exploration of guilt:
    I think I am bad for having eaten too much cake. I say I want to lose weight, but sometimes I can't help but be indulgent.

    Example of exploration of shame:
    I think I am a fat, indulgent, ugly pig. I don't like the way I look or who I am.

    Example of a deeper exploration of shame:
    I am too big, I take up too much space. I don't deserve to be here. I am a mistake.

3. Once you have identified the judgments, ask yourself, "Am I ready to let this go and heal?" If your answer is "yes," write your forgiveness statements.

Examples:

I forgive myself for believing myself to be bad.

I forgive myself for calling myself a fat, pig.

I forgive myself for judging myself as unworthy.

I forgive myself for buying into the notion that I am a mistake.

4. Focus your awareness on your heart. Let your attention settle there and say your forgiveness statements out loud.

Examples:

I forgive myself for judging myself as bad.

I forgive myself for calling myself a fat, pig.

I forgive myself for judging myself as unworthy.

I forgive myself for judging myself as a mistake

5. After you feel complete with your forgiveness statements, create your new truth statements from your heart or from your Higher Self.

Examples:

The truth is I am not a pig. I'm a bit overweight and intend to start my new eating program soon. (Remember, if you can change it great, if not accept it!)

The truth is I love chocolate cake and eating it makes me very happy. When I am ready to commit, focus and imple-

ment my new health regiment I will! Until then I'm going to thoroughly enjoy my chocolate cake!

The truth is I am worthy!

The truth is I am not a mistake!

Other examples of truth statements:

The truth is I am profoundly valuable and I deserve love.

The truth is I am as God created me.

The truth is I am a child of God and am loved and loveable.

The truth is I am a spiritual being having a human experience and I am wonderful, precious and divine!

People who experience extreme guilt or shame often want to hide. They do not want to be seen or talk about how they feel. It is a lonely and painful experience. However, we must be seen, understood and accepted by ourselves and others in order to heal. This is why support groups such as 12-step programs can be extraordinarily helpful, especially when shame is coupled with addiction.

As mentioned in the previous chapter, we can choose to focus on the good or bad, the guilt or innocence. As you release guilt and shame, negative self-identification will loosen its grip on you. You will experience a profound state of freedom and relief. It can be experienced as a deep relaxation and comfort in the body.

Ancient scriptures consistently assure us the essence of who we are as humans is pure, beautiful and without stain. The essence of who you are is indeed exquisite and extraordinary. Once you remember and embrace this truth, not only will you feel more confident and peaceful, but true love will naturally, gracefully and easily show up in your life.

Chapter 9.
Emotions

*To give vent now and then to his feelings, whether of pleasure
or discontent, is a great ease to a man's heart.*
~ *Francesco Guicciardini*

*Let us not forget that the little emotions are the great captains
of our lives and we obey them without realizing it.*
~ *Vincent Van Gogh*

Emotions can be a powerful indication of our connection
to Spirit or our Higher Self. They are an important gateway in
our evolution and spiritual development. Feelings are the way
our soul speaks to our minds and bodies. Giving credence to
our feelings is imperative if we want to live in optimal physical,
mental, emotional and spiritual health. When we understand
and honor our emotions, not only are we more cognizant of
who we are, we also create a strong foundation for a healthy
relationship with ourselves and therefore with others.

Emovere is the Latin root for emotion and means "to
move." *Emotion* can be translated to literally mean "energy in
motion." Our thoughts assist us in creating our reality.
Additionally, our emotions are powerful motivators and an
incredible energy source. Imagine your thoughts and beliefs are
like a car and engine. Keeping this imagery in mind, feelings
and emotions are akin to the horsepower and fuel.

When thoughts, beliefs and emotions are not aligned, life can be chaotic and confusing. When our thoughts, beliefs and emotions are aligned and focused in a negative direction, life can be painful and challenging. When our thoughts, beliefs and emotions are aligned and moving in a *positive* direction, miracles happen!

Emotions guide us. They let us know if we are on track or have lost our way. They let us know whether or not we are in alignment with our Higher Self. Feelings are our inner compass. Without them, we would not be attuned to our intuition, be clear about our direction, or feel in sync with life.

All emotions have vital information for us. Certain emotions such as anger, sadness and fear have a bad reputation, especially for those on a spiritual path. These emotions are not the problem; it is the repression and denial of these emotions that create our biggest challenges and cause our greatest pain. Bypassing or suppressing difficult emotions is usually ineffective and often destructive.

Denied or ignored feelings do not go away. The energy of emotion remains stored in the body where it continues to fester. This energy can create blocks and cause you to experience depression, a nervous breakdown or physical crisis.

Buried feelings will eventually surface and manifest in some way. Every thought and emotion we experience sends a message to the cells in our body. Some messages are louder than others, but communication is continually taking place.

Most of us learn by the age of four or five to suppress or camouflage our true feelings. Consequently, it becomes challenging or impossible for us to be sensitive and mindful of them as adults. Our family of origin may not have wanted to hear what we were thinking or feeling. For example, many of us heard, "Big kids don't cry." Certain restrictions in society made it difficult to articulate our truth. We were led to believe that if we could turn off our feelings, things would be better. When our feelings were discounted, disallowed or when our hurt was simply too much to process, many of us became emotionally disconnected or numb in order to cope.

Many times throughout my childhood I heard the phrase, "I don't care what you think or what you feel! Just do what you're told!" I thought if I could stop feeling, it would be easier to be a good girl and, therefore, be loved. It seemed to work for a while, only to backfire later. We pay a high price when we attempt to stop feeling. We lose touch with our truth and our guidance system. As a result, pain takes up residence in our emotional and physical bodies.

Our sense of safety in the world is generally established when we are young. It is a significant contributing factor in the creation of our emotional baseline. Is the world a loving place or is it a scary place? Do you trust the process of life or does it frighten you? Do you adapt to change well or do you find it terrifying? If you believe the universe is a loving and supportive place, it is easier to flow with life. You connect with others, trust yourself and are more comfortable with your feelings.

When I was first asked, "Do you think the universe is a safe and loving place or not?" my immediate response was "absolutely not!" I was afraid of life and tried to resist and control it. Being constantly nervous, I was always on my guard. I had a history of being betrayed and no longer trusted anyone. For a long time, I suppressed and denied my feelings. This resulted in confusion and depression. I was numb and did not feel, value or trust my emotions. Bizarre and dramatic events occurred within my relationships and there seemed to be a great deal of anger coming at me. I was out of balance and my life was reflecting it back to me in a powerful way.

I was out of touch with my internal guidance system and out of alignment with my Higher Self. I wondered if I was too far gone to ever find my way back. During meditation, I had a vision that we each have a rope that permanently connects us to Spirit. In my depressed and fearful state, I was literally at the end of my rope. I then realized as long as we are still breathing the opportunity for healing still exists. Living in my head and trying to figure things out was not only painful, it was simply not working. I knew I needed to get in touch with my heart and my feelings if I was ever going to be happy and find my way home.

Processing Guilt

A teacher once mentioned I seemed to be carrying a great deal of unexpressed grief. It was true and I felt tears behind my eyes as she said it. However, I had no idea what to do about it. She suggested an exercise that would help me to release my grief. I needed to get some organic onions, chop them up, bundle them in a warm wet cloth and place it on my chest. Next, I was to breathe deeply and let the process unfold. I thought it sounded strange, but I decided I would give it a try.

I purchased my supplies, chopped the onions, ran my fabric under warm water, wrung it out and prepared for my adventure with the onions. I wrote a prayer to Spirit and asked for support, guidance and healing. Then, I lit a candle, blessed my "sacred onions," and let the situation unfold.

I had no idea what to expect, but shortly after I placed the concoction on my chest the fumes hit and tears began to flow. After a few minutes, a torrential downpour ensued. As I cried, I saw images. Memories surfaced from my recent past with Bob, as well as some from childhood. I allowed the memories and the tears to move through me without trying to hold on to, direct or analyze anything. It felt as if I was riding a huge wave.

About an hour later, the tears started to slow down and they eventually stopped. I always thought I would feel worse if I allowed myself to cry. However, when I finally gave myself permission to release the tears and actually feel my sadness, I felt better, lighter and somehow cleansed.

My emotional energy had been blocked for a very long time. I suffered from chronic fatigue and serious health problems for many years. I believe a large part of my physical challenges, lack of energy and depression was caused by suppressed grief. I also came to realize I was unable to feel happiness and joy because I denied and disowned my sorrow. Feelings that have not been felt, processed or resolved unconsciously govern our thoughts, beliefs, health and relationships. Emotions that are buried and ignored can affect every aspect of our lives.

Although I now had access to my sadness, this emotion was not alone. I found beneath my grief, there was anger; beneath the anger, there was more sadness. As an adult, I never found the prospect of anger or sadness appealing. However, of these two emotions, sadness seemed more acceptable. Anger was simply not allowed in my family and I decided as a child anger should be renounced. When I decided to embark upon my spiritual path, I believed anger was unacceptable and unspiritual. However, in my studies and through my healing process, I learned that the energy of anger is important, valuable and even necessary.

Ultimately, anger is about boundaries and protection. Anger protects your individuality and lets others know when they have crossed the line. Anger serves you when you have been disrespected or when you witness others being suppressed or controlled. If you do not have access to your anger, you will inevitably be taken advantage of and become a victim. It is by listening to, allowing and expressing your anger that your sense of self can be protected or restored.

Many believe they are doing a good job of suppressing their anger, or they may not realize they have any negative emotions to process at all. However, life will always reflect back to us any disowned or repressed aspects of ourselves. Suppressed emotions do not go away; they simply "leak out" in confusing, uncomfortable and unfortunate ways. For example; if you do not own and express your anger, you will most likely encounter or be confronted by angry people.

Jeff's Story

My friend Jeff had several relationships with overtly angry women. He also had history of being pulled over by the police—even if he was not breaking the law. He seemed to always be getting in trouble with women and figures of authority. I found his situation interesting and somewhat odd. As we talked about Jeff's situation, it was eventually revealed how much anger he had accumulated over the years. His anger started with his original authority figures— his mother and father. On the surface, it seemed like he and his parents had a pretty good relationship. However, he had disowned many of his feelings because he did not believe expressing them was mature or acceptable.

Jeff decided to undergo therapy and began to get in touch with his feelings. Once he allowed himself to feel, process and express his suppressed emotions, healing started to occur. The confrontational and aggressive experiences in his life started to shift and dissipate. Overtly angry females and angry policeman became part of his past. Jeff is now more in touch with his feelings. He has since manifested a wonderful relationship with a very kind woman. He also has not been approached by a police officer in more than three years!

When you start to feel angry, ask yourself "What needs to be protected?" or "What needs to be restored?" Anger contains intense energy that is vital to physical, mental, emotional and spiritual health. When we suppress, bury or deny anger, it can result in apathy, depression and boundary invasion. As my friend Jeff will attest, anger can also come at you from outside sources.

Rage is an explosion of anger. It can occur when we experience an extremely threatening situation or when our anger has been building for a long time. Rage can be positive if channeled and focused to help define our boundaries as long as we do not inflict it on anyone. This emotion can carry intense power, energy and information. However, if not properly dealt with, rage can cause significant damage to ourselves and others. If rage burns out of control or is constant, it is imperative to contact a mental health professional. We cannot strengthen ourselves, or become healthy by either repressing our anger or running wild with it.

Sadness is another misunderstood and frequently disowned emotion. Sadness is often considered unacceptable or negative—especially for men. It carries the perception of being vulnerable, unstable or weak. Sadness and anger can be intertwined. Often people who lead with sadness (unexpressed anger) end up in relationships with people who lead with anger (unexpressed sadness). This is the recipe for victim-abuser relationships.

It is in everyone's best interest to be able to feel and process all of their emotions. When we refuse to feel our sadness, we lose focus and our ability to go with the flow. Stress, tension, anger and dysfunctional relationships will follow. When we experience and accept our sadness, we come to realize what needs to be changed, expressed or released. It helps us to slow down, feel our losses and cultivate compassion for ourselves and others. Tears can also relieve stress, which can be caused by a surplus of chemicals created by strong repressed feelings. This is why suppressing our tears and our sadness is not good for our bodies. Gary Zukav, author of *Seat of the Soul* says, "Tears are the healing balm of the soul." Acknowledging and releasing sadness can restore our balance and sense of wholeness if we simply allow it to exist.

I am reminded of a story. A young student encounters his teacher, an enlightened master. One of the master's friends died and he was crying. The student asked, "If you are so 'evolved,' why are you crying?" The teacher answered, "I am crying because I am sad."

It can be that simple. Just because we are "evolved" does not mean we no longer experience emotions. Feelings will be our constant companion on our human journey.

Fear also has gotten a bad rap, especially in certain spiritual beliefs. If we cultivate a healthy relationship with it, this emotion can be a good friend. Vital information can be embedded in our fear. It can alert us to danger and change; it can keep us focused, aware and out of harm's way. Fear can help us act on our instincts and intuition. Do not confuse fear with anxiety, worry, panic and terror, which occur when someone is overwhelmed or disconnected. These emotions may also occur when fear has been unheeded or if boundaries are impaired.

For a great deal of my life, I experienced anxiety, panic and even terror from simply walking out of my house. Getting coffee, shopping or just encountering another human being was often alarming. I was in constant pain because of my very weak boundaries. Fear had stepped forward and took over my life. I realize now my disproportionate fear was simply an unconscious alert system attempting to protect me.

Strengthening my boundaries has been vital in creating a healthy relationship with myself. My relationship with fear is now more positive and balanced. I now experience fear as intuition or a gut feeling. It assists me in processing information. Fear also helps me to respond to the environment and circumstances. I will sometimes experience fear as I am driving on the freeways in Los Angeles. My healthy fear has alerted me to flying hubcaps, debris in the road and unsafe drivers.

As I was walking through a crowded restaurant with a friend one evening, I quickly stepped to the side for no apparent reason. Coincidentally (or maybe not, depending on how you look at it), this happened just as a man tried to grab me. I eluded him without a second to spare. Astonished, my friend said I looked like a bat in a cave. She wondered how I knew the man was going to do that, after all I had not seen him. I smiled and told her, "My radar is working, I just felt it."

When we have a healthy relationship with fear, just like any other human emotion, it shows up when we need it. It supports us in dealing with what is going on at the moment. We can then release it and move on. If we suppress or deny this important energy, it can come up at inappropriate times and at a disproportionate level. If we do not understand or accept our fear, we will not have access to our instincts or intuition. Fear can be like a flashing yellow light asking us to be aware, prepare ourselves and act consciously.

Happiness and joy are expansive emotions that most of us strive for and are usually considered spiritual, acceptable and positive. If you close off or disallow the emotions at the "negative" end of emotional spectrum, you will not be capable of experiencing the emotions at the "positive" end. You cannot experience authentic happiness, peace or joy if you do not give yourself permission to feel your sadness, fear, anger and grief. It is important to honor all of your emotions or your life will become dreary and stagnant.

Many of us wrongly believe happiness is achieved by something external. Our society thrives on chasing happiness and the art of distraction. We are inundated by information, images and options that make hollow promises of happiness and fulfillment. Technology has given us an abundance of opportunities to distract us from ourselves. The truth is this: nothing outside ourselves can make us happy for long. The only reason we desire anything outside of ourselves is because of how we believe it will make us *feel*. It is through our feelings that every external event is filtered and experienced. This can be a very liberating concept because it means nothing is required outside of ourselves in order to know inner peace, contentment and joy.

Happiness is an internal experience. For it to be authentic, we need to stop running from ourselves; we need to pay attention to our bodies and *feel*. Happiness is indeed a wonderful experience and happens spontaneously and easily when we clear out our trapped emotional energies.

Emotions are the soul's language. If you try to banish any emotion you perceive to be unacceptable, you ignore the message your soul is attempting to communicate. One of my teachers once told me, "Beneath anger is hurt; beneath hurt is love." By giving credence to our anger and having compassion for our hurt, we eventually get to the place of love, peace and equanimity within. When we clear out our repressed emotions, they will arise only when needed and we will be able to express them in a healthy way. They will move through us and be released once they have served their rightful purpose.

With the help of emotions, we can become extremely resourceful, highly intuitive and authentically empowered. When we welcome, respect and trust our feelings, we connect to the deepest part of ourselves and increase our capacity for authentic connections with others.

Exercise: Allowing and Releasing Emotions

One of the most healing gifts you can give yourself is to grant full permission to experience and express your emotions. A powerful technique I use to process and rid myself of disturbing emotions is "Stream of Consciousness Writing." The next time you find yourself experiencing unpleasant emotions, use this process. You can also use it to release stress or tension in your body and allow it to communicate through your writing. For example, let the tension in your shoulders express what they are feeling or give the tightness in your gut a voice.

1. Create a sacred space where you can write without interruption. If you like, light a candle or burn some incense. Turn off the ringer on your phone. Advise your loved ones that you would like some private time and be left undisturbed until you complete this process.

2. Gather several sheets of loose writing paper and some pens or pencils. It is most beneficial to do Stream of Consciousness Writing by hand rather than on a computer or typewriter.

3. Set a clear intention to release any emotional discomfort and any feelings that are no longer serving you. Give yourself wholehearted permission to express your emotions in writing without editing or censoring. Allow yourself to begin the writing process with whatever is present no matter how disturbing or silly it may seem. Do not worry about how legible the writing is. You do not have to be able to read or interpret it. If you are angry or upset, you may find that your style of writing changes. You may end up even scribbling or scratching at the paper. Through this process you may experience

and express many different types of emotions and memories. This is all fine. Simply allow the process to be what it is and follow where it takes you.

4. Continue writing for as long as you feel charged. It is *very important* that you do not reread anything that you have written. This process is about dispelling, discharging and releasing negative and painful emotions. You do not want to reintroduce any of this energy back into your body and psyche.

5 You may find as you continue with this process you experience insights, revelations or creative ideas. Have another sheet of paper (or your journal) available to capture in writing any creative ideas or valuable information you may want to keep. If your negative emotion returns, you may then go back to the paper you are using for the Stream of Consciousness Writing. This way, you honor your process as it unfolds. You will most likely find a natural completion to your flow often accompanied by a sense of relief and sometimes even poetry.

6. Once you have listened to yourself and processed your emotions you may be complete. This is accompanied by a sense of peace and relaxation in your body. If you are still tense, negative emotions are still present. You can invite your Inner Child forward and ask if there is anything else he or she wants to say. What does he or she need to feel better? This process should gracefully bring your process to completion.

7. When you reach completion, gather up the loose papers you have written on and burn them in a safe manner. Another option is to shred the loose pages into small pieces and dispose of them. The ritual of burning or

destroying what you have written symbolizes and assists you in releasing your negative energy. This is a powerful and essential step in the Stream of Consciousness Writing Exercise.

This exercise becomes even more effective when performed consistently over a number of days. For example, you may choose to do at least 20 or more minutes of Stream of Consciousness Writing every day for a week to effectively support yourself in moving, expressing and releasing challenging emotions.

When we know how to acknowledge, process and release our negative or suppressed emotions, we no longer look at others through the distorted filter of our unexpressed pain. We no longer need others to behave differently so we can feel better. When we know how to take responsibility for our own emotions, we become emotionally independent and we become spiritual adults. We communicate more clearly and in a more empowered fashion. We also live a life of greater peace and clarity. Owning, understanding and processing our emotions supports us in being authentic. This is the solid foundation for any healthy relationship and necessary for a true soul-to-soul connection with another human being.

Chapter 10
People Pleasing

A 'No' uttered from the deepest conviction is better than a 'Yes' merely uttered to please, or worse, to avoid trouble.
~Mohandas Gandhi

Living the truth in your heart without compromise brings kindness into the world. Attempts at kindness that compromise your heart cause only sadness.
~Anonymous 18th century monk

As humans, we all want to be respected, loved and acknowledged by others. However, if we have an overwhelming need for these experiences, it is easy to fall into a pattern where we sacrifice ourselves to earn approval from others. Something I found to be vital in manifesting and maintaining balanced, loving, healthy relationships, is the ability to take care of my own needs first. In my practice, I frequently see people who have a tendency to take care of the needs of others before considering their own. They are known as *People Pleasers*. To determine if you or someone you know has a tendency to please, consider the following questions:

Is taking care of others important to you?

Is the experience of being wanted or needed important to you?

Do you often put others' needs before your own?

Do you think you need to be perfect to be loved?

Are you deeply affected by what others think of you?

Do you change your behavior to ensure others' happiness?

Do you avoid conflict, challenge or controversy?

Are you afraid to speak your truth?

Do you have difficulty asking for what you want or need?

Are you out of touch with your feelings?

Do you have trouble saying no?

Do you experience chronic guilt?

Do you take on too much responsibility or too many projects?

Do you need to be in relationship to feel complete?

Have you experienced significant pain in relationships?

Do you have a history of being abandoned or betrayed?

If you answered yes to more than three or four of these questions, you probably tend to be a People Pleaser. Often the unconscious goal of a Pleaser is to care for others in order to feel a sense of value and worth, as well as to avoid rejection, disappointment or criticism.

Self-sacrifice and compromise can be a natural part of a healthy relationship. Wanting to care for others and to put their happiness in front of your own, on occasion, can be considered generous and virtuous. However, caring for others can end up being destructive if it is at the expense of caring for yourself. If you sacrifice being true to who you are, in order to spare hurting the feelings of someone else, or if you make other people's lives a priority over your own, eventually your relationships will result in significant pain.

Pleasers usually appear quite pleasant, helpful and kind. They are more comfortable giving than receiving. The downside is that Pleasers are usually out of touch with their own needs, desires, preferences, opinions and feelings. They have a problem saying "no" and often end up taking on too much. Pleasers frequently extend themselves to an uncomfortable and sometimes impossible degree.

People Pleasers can experience a slowly mounting sense of frustration and resentment. They keep saying "yes" with a smile on their face. However, if they were honest, they would say "no." They neglect their own needs while caring for others to such a degree, they eventually end up feeling depleted. I have seen Pleasers eventually snap, like the proverbial straw that breaks the camel's back, they become disproportionately upset over a relatively small situation. People around them are often confused by this behavior because the Pleasers generally set up the precedent and balance (or imbalance) within the relationship in the first place.

Pleasers can also turn anger and frustration inward. This may be acted out in self-abusive, passive-aggressive or unconscious ways. Pleasers frequently have a propensity toward addictions or obsessive compulsive behaviors. Health challenges are almost always an issue; taking on too much can obviously cause discomfort, stress, exhaustion and dis-ease. Pleasers are like chameleons as they conform and contort themselves into what they believe others want or expect. This can cause great discomfort mentally, emotionally, physically and spiritually. They are disconnected from their true emotions and out of alignment with their Higher Self.

Pleasers can be very sensitive and empathetic, to the point they actually feel another's pain. They may consciously or unconsciously take on someone else's discomfort. Pleasers may find it difficult, if not impossible, to differentiate between their own pain and that of a loved one.

It may seem like a contradiction, but Pleasers can actually be very self-centered and controlling. Although they may sacrifice themselves to keep everyone happy, what they actually want is for everyone to be happy with *them*. They believe they should be capable of taking care of others' moods and experiences. If things are not going well, or if people are unhappy, Pleasers will become distressed as they try to put order into their environment. In a Pleaser's mind, he or she is responsible for the thoughts, needs, experiences and feelings of others. If they do not succeed, they feel guilty, inadequate, frustrated, angry or depressed. This is an unrealistic goal and an impossible burden to carry indefinitely. Pleasers have a sense of being overly responsible for circumstances and the people around them. Often this is unconsciously coupled with a distorted and exaggerated sense of importance and power.

Pleasers tend to take inventory of the moods and behaviors from the people around them, rather than managing and being aware of their own. They are guided by external reference points to determine how they are doing and what their value is. People Pleasers often lack a solid sense of self and can be out of touch with their internal compass. They may seem ungrounded, nervous, anxious or appear to be uncomfortable in their own skin. After all, controlling everything and everyone around you can be a very uncomfortable place to be!

I was a People Pleaser in the extreme and healing this dynamic was not easy. My identity and sense of worth was wrapped up in those around me. I felt it was my responsibility to take care of other people. Feeling I had given all I had to give to a relationship only to be completely dismissed without closure left me feeling completely disoriented and devalued. I went into a deep depression and felt confused about who I was and my life's purpose. Who was I if I was not the person who cared for my fiancé and our friends? When that relationship deteriorated, my identity and direction in life completely evaporated. I had no solid internal foudation or sense of power. I had no idea who I was or what I was supposed to be doing.

Adding insult to injury, a friend said to me that by attempting to be the Pleaser in that relationship I was a liar. I could not figure out what she meant or how that could be true. All I had done was make another person important in my reality! How could I be a liar? I felt what my friend said was inaccurate, mean-spirited and rude. (Of course, I did not say it out loud, that would not be nice!). After pondering what she said, I realized there may be some truth in it. I did agree to things I did not want to do. I allowed myself to be swept along in situations and circumstances that made my stomach hurt. I said things were fine when they were not. I smiled when I was sad. In addition, I frequently sacrificed things that mattered very much to me.

When I had gotten as far away from myself as I could possibly get, the very thin strand that had connected my fiancé and me finally snapped. The opportunity for real healing was about to begin. I had been abandoned, betrayed and emotionally abused. All of this was because I abandoned, betrayed and emotionally abused myself. The truth is this: no one can treat you worse than you treat yourself. When you have an overwhelming desire to please others rather than to honor yourself, there will inevitably be self-sacrifice, betrayal, lies and dishonesty. It all starts when you betray and lie to yourself.

I realized I had gotten pretty far off track. I knew I had a choice to make—either stay off track and slip into oblivion or pull myself up by the bootstraps and set my intention to heal. I became conscious of the fact I needed to address my tendency to please. I knew I wanted to be happy and whole within myself. I also wanted to help others and be of service. However, first, I had to address my own personal pain, trauma and drama. I had no idea what it was going to take, but I set the intention to find the courage to heal and always take that next step. The journey from self-destruction and self-loathing to Self-love and authentic power seemed daunting and overwhelming, but I understood it had to be done.

I believe when we express a strong desire or state an intention, the Universe hears us and conspires to support us. Soon after setting my intention I was intuitively drawn to certain classes and began my formal education. Of course, the school of life also continued to support my intention to evolve and heal. I was indeed being presented with a buffet of educational and soul-expanding opportunities.

One of the deeply ingrained habits I wanted to shift was my need to take responsibility for others. I decided it was time to "till my own land." What that meant to me was simply to be responsible for myself and not try to fix other people's problems. What a novel concept! Do not get into other people's gardens and try to take care of it for them. Do not fertilize their ground, pull their weeds or pick their flowers. Do not tell them what or how they should plant and do not give advice unless asked. Plant your own flowers and take care of your own little piece of the world. If you do a good job, you will be given more. And maybe the guy with the garden next door will ask for some of your healthy tomato secrets!

By "tilling my own land" and creating my own wonderful life, I eventually became happy and whole. I realized I could care for myself and others and be of great service by simply focusing on living my "best life." When others observed how well I was doing and how I was succeeding in the world, people started to ask, "How did you do it?" and "What is your secret?"

If you have ever traveled on an airplane, you are probably familiar with the safety instruction flight attendants share: "In the event of an emergency, put your oxygen mask on first before assisting others." This is a wonderful literal and metaphoric analogy. If we do not care for ourselves first, we will not be of any great value to anybody else.

God gave each of us the most extraordinary creative medium—life. We can make out of it whatever we choose, but we must remember to keep our attention on our own work of art! I believe it is our biggest responsibility. This is why gossip and over involvement in others' lives can be so destructive. You are not taking responsibility for your creative medium when you are mucking around in *someone else's life*. How is this good for you or other people? Get back into your own experience! Tighten up your boundaries! Focus on your place in the world! Be thankful for what you have and for who you are. You were given much and you can have so much more with the attitude of gratitude and when you take responsibility for yourself.

Another wonderful revelation I had was the awareness that God is in other people, too! I do not need to take care of everyone. I do not need to know what anyone else needs. What a relief! I started to relax knowing I did not have to take care of anyone or make them better. Each one of us is personally linked to Spirit and our own guidance system, even if we do not know it yet. Those who do not will eventually figure out what is best for them, even if it does not seem right from anyone else's perspective.

Debbie's Story

I had a good friend, Debbie, who I thought was making an "interesting" choice in a relationship. It seemed that the man she was dating had a few demons in his closet and he drank a lot. I often thought he was on his best behavior and was trying to trap her into a relationship. However, I knew God was in Debbie and she was capable of making her own choices. I thought, "Who knows what her soul is trying to learn? Besides, what do I really know about their relationship?" I decided to let her be. As the relationship progressed, they did indeed, have a great deal to teach and learn from one another.

It is easy to sit on the outside looking in and think we know what is best for the people we care about. When we love someone, we often form opinions about how they should handle things. However, we must remember their life is their creative medium, just as your life is your creative medium.

When I talked to Debbie about her relationship, I set the intention to simply love and support her while she made her own decisions. She was happy, optimistic and pleased to be communicating about her current situation. My intention was to accept her completely. I simply honored and respected her process. This was a very freeing and liberating experience for me. I knew she was going to do what she felt she needed to do and I did not need to know, do or fix anything!

Debbie's marriage lasted less than one year. After her divorce, she shared with me some of the difficulties she experienced. In the past, I would have felt compelled to give her advice. I might have also felt guilty, thinking I was the one who could have saved her from heartache. But not now! I was now free to be me and allow her the freedom to be her. I simply allowed Debbie to have her own experience and hold her in my heart. She had some shame about her relationship not working out the way she had hoped. I encouraged her to share the things she had learned. I then shared with her my perspective of the positive transformation I had witnessed in her. Over the course of Debbie's relationship, I observed that she became more confident and

aware of her power; she had also cultivated stronger boundaries. Debbie agreed. She thanked me for not judging her
and acknowledged that the experience was not all bad.

By supporting Debbie and focusing on the very best in her
and her situation, Debbie went from embarrassment over her
failed marriage and disappointment in herself to acknowledging
that she did what she thought was best. I told Debbie that this
man was probably the perfect "teacher" for her and she
learned important life lessons by virtue of this relationship.
Because of her involvement with him, Debbie was now more
solid, evolved and confident.

When Debbie is ready for her next relationship, she will
better understand what she wants. I believe the process of dating, relationships and life is about refining our intentions and
desires. By virtue of our experiences—good and bad—we have
the opportunity to become clear about what we want and do
not want. Once we know what we want in a relationship, we
can easily focus our energy, set our intentions and attract it!

Giving Advice versus Listening

If someone does not ask for your opinion or advice, he or
she probably does not want it and will not hear it. Giving
advice when it is not invited can cause discomfort, defensive-
ness and resentment. It can also make someone feel like he or
she is being told what to do or judged (even when your advice
is given with the best of intentions and with love in your
heart). Asking questions and listening works much better than
advice. This allows a person to look deeper into his or her
experience. Asking questions supports another person in
exploring and expressing his or her truth. Listening is a wonderful and highly underrated skill. Brenda Ueland, a prolific
journalist, editor, freelance writer and teacher, says, "Listening

is a magnetic and strange thing, a creative force. When people really listen to each other in a quiet, fascinated attention, the creative fountain inside each of us begins to spring and cast up new thoughts and unexpected wisdom." Heartfelt listening is one of the most powerful gifts we can give to another. Not only does it make them feel cared for, but creates the space for them to tap into the divine wisdom within.

We never know what another person's soul is trying to learn. To think we know what is best for anyone is not only exhausting, but impossible. We all have our own individual "contracts"—what we agreed to before we were born on this planet. It is our job to align and find *our* purpose and learn *our* lessons. No one can do it for us and we cannot do it for anyone else. All we can do is love others unconditionally while they go through their process of sifting and sorting out their truth.

If it gets to a point where it pains you too much to witness a loved one's seemingly self-destructive choices rather than telling them what to do, tell them it hurts you to see them exhibiting certain behaviors. If it continues, you may have to remove yourself from the situation in order to preserve your alignment and connection with Spirit. This is where boundaries come in. Although this may sound manipulative or insensitive, you are actually caring for yourself.

A powerful statement that I use and have shared with other Pleasers is, "It's not my problem." Although this may initially seem uncaring, it really is not. It is the ability to discern our boundaries and take personal responsibility without taking over responsibility for someone else. It also supports others as they work through their issues and lessons.

I recall a time when I was traveling with my husband, Steve, who is generally good natured and sweet. However, on this particular day, he was tired, irritable and hungry. As we were going through security at an airport, some people cut into the line in front of us. Steve was at the end of his rope and started snapping at people. I tried to joke with him, take care of him, cajole him and comfort him. Nothing worked. Steve seemed determined to be grouchy.

After Steve and I made it through security I said, "Steve, you know I love you, but I cannot change how you are feeling. I am not abandoning you, but I am going to take care of myself now. Please know that I am here for you, if and when you are ready." I went to the newsstand, bought a magazine and sat by the gate and read. A little later, my husband joined me. He thanked me for giving him the space to work through his frustration and anger. By me making the choice to take care of myself, it allowed Steve to take care of himself. He was able to put things into perspective and was ready to reconnect with me from a more balanced and peaceful place.

In my past relationships, if my partner was in an uncomfortable place, I would be right there with him. If he was in a deep, dark well I would go down there too. I would do anything and everything I could to try and pull him out of it and make him feel better. I often ended up depleted, sick and completely stressed out. The worst part of this was even though I was willing to sacrifice myself for the other person, it did not help. To top things off, there was nothing left of me. I wanted to reach down and pull them up, but instead they pulled me down!

Now that I have become a priority in my own life, I can more effectively take care of others. I care for them in right amounts in appropriate ways, and I feel good! This is an example of setting boundaries. I do not go into the well for someone else and I do not ask them to go there for me. I maintain sovereignty within myself and make my connection to my center and Spirit my first priority.

When you truly commit to taking better care of yourself, you can then take better care of others. When you love yourself it is easy to see the best in other people. You naturally focus on their positive qualities, praise them and see through the "eyes of love". This is what really pleases people!

The people who truly please are those who are so at home within themselves, they simply allow others to be their own unique selves. They listen to others, ask questions and let them be where they are. They are empathetic and give others the room to explore, experience and enjoy who they are. When we can do this our relationships are fulfilling, supportive, expansive and exquisite. As Carl Rogers, an influential psychologist and one of the founders of the humanistic approach once said, "People are just as extraordinary, unique and beautiful as sunsets—if you'll let them be."

Exercise: Shifting from People Pleasing to Personal Authenticity

1. Take a few minutes to write down two or three situations in your life in which you might easily fall into the pattern of People Pleasing or taking more than your fair share of responsibility.

    Example: *Saying yes to someone who invites me on a date even though it doesn't really feel right for me.*

    Example: *Going to an appointment I don't feel up to instead of rescheduling or canceling it altogether.*

    Example: *I have extended an invitation to a few friends for a barbeque and am now feeling overwhelmed by the amount of work that I have to do.*

2. With each situation you have listed, write what is true for you regardless of how you think the other person or people might feel or respond. What would be the self-honoring choice, action or statement in each case?

   Example: *My intuition clearly told me that this person is not someone I am not really interested in. The self-honoring choice would be to cancel the date.*

   Example: I *woke up this morning and really felt I needed to take some time for myself. The self-honoring choice would be to change the appointment to another day.*

   Example: *When I invited people over for a barbeque, I did not know my week was going to be so hectic and busy. The self-honoring choice would be to make it a pot luck dinner and ask each person to bring one item, so I don't have to do all the work by myself.*

Keys for Becoming True to Yourself

1. Become conscious and aware of any People Pleasing tendencies you may have and then set the intention to be more true to yourself.

2. Learning to say, "no thank you," "that is not good for me," or "that does not honor me" are powerful and important statements when it is true for you.

3. Saying "yes, please" when someone offers assistance is a wonderful step in the right direction.

4. Be willing to be more honest, open and release the need for perfection.

5. When facing an important decision or when you are not sure of what to do next, take a moment to ask yourself, "What is best for me?" or "What honors me now?"

6. Balance is achieved as we learn to speak up on our own behalf, have the courage to tell our truth, establish boundaries and are willing to explore our individuality.

7. Freedom is experienced when we release expectations and let go of feeling responsible for other people's lives—including bad moods and disappointments.

8. We benefit significantly when we start to cultivate humor and compassion for ourselves.

9. As People Pleasers, what we need more than anything is simply permission from ourselves to be wonderfully, awesomely, authentically human!

I still love taking care of others and making my friends and family smile. The difference now is I also love taking care of me. I no longer exhaust myself in the process of giving and caretaking. My equilibrium and internal balance is maintained by taking the time to check in and ask myself this very important question, "What honors me now?"

I am clear in my boundaries and I live in my truth. I share from my abundance and overflow and am aware of how much I can give before I step over the line into deficit and depletion. I have become a priority in my own life and feel more whole, happy and more authentically generous than I have ever felt before!

Chapter 11
Boundaries

If the boulders are moved, even a river will change its flow.
~ Taoism

Freedom is greatest when the boundaries are clearly defined.
~ Chuck Coonradt

In the physical world, boundaries are easy to see—fences, walls, roads, signs, seashores and cliffs clearly mark the limits of society and nature. We can see our physical body's boundaries by virtue of our skin. However, in the realm of energy and emotions, they can be much more difficult to define. Energetic and emotional boundaries are a clearly defined sense of self. Our sense of boundaries allows us to acknowledge and respect the differences, preferences, feelings, beliefs and experiences of ourselves and others.

Boundaries are important in all relationships, including those with our romantic partners, business colleagues, families, friends, neighbors, pets, children and even strangers. Understanding and implementing them supports us in celebrating and honoring the uniqueness of ourselves and other people. If we were not taught to understand and establish healthy boundaries early in life, they can be challenging—although not impossible—to cultivate later on.

Parents often find encouraging a healthy sense of boundaries to be a complex and challenging task. One reason is because we develop different types of them during the five stages of development that range from infancy to early adulthood. Here is a brief description of each stage of development:

Infancy (up to age 1). Infants see the world as an extension of themselves. They cannot comprehend the concept of boundaries and do not intentionally violate them. It is important for parents to frequently touch and hold their infants while showering them with attention. When a parent mirrors and echoes their baby's behavior both verbally and nonverbally, they give the child a signal that the parent is there for them. Mirroring and echoing makes the infant feel safe and understood.

The Toddler Years (ages 1 to 3). Toddlers start to comprehend the concept of "self" and "other." They need consistent and simple communication to assist in the creation of boundaries, such as "sit down," "don't bite," and "don't touch—it's hot!" When toddlers learn to express themselves with "no!" they are making early attempts at creating their own boundaries. Guidance, patience, unconditional love and nurturing are vital as children begin to develop boundaries and grow emotionally.

Preschoolers (ages 4 to 6). Parents of preschoolers should stay calm when their child "acts out" in order to test boundaries. They can offer support by providing advice, assistance and other forms of verbal and nonverbal help. Appropriate behaviors need to be taught and modeled by parents. This helps preschoolers to comprehend and create healthy social skills. Children's feelings should be allowed and validated so they can have the freedom to experience their authentic selves. It is important that children are allowed to play and be creative so they can learn about their boundaries. They need love, approval and acceptance in order to fulfill their potential.

School-aged children (ages 6 to 13). School-aged children require consistent boundaries and need to understand boundaries have been set to keep them protected and safe. They should be aware boundaries are non-negotiable and they will receive consequences if they do not respect them. Children need to be heard, understood and accepted. At this age, they also need to experience loyalty and trust. Children must be allowed to feel and express their emotions, including grieving their losses through to completion. Accepting appropriate responsibility, receiving validation for accomplishments and completing tasks with the support and guidance of parents are all important aspects of comprehending and implementing boundaries.

Adolescents (ages 13 to 18). Adolescents will need new boundaries established as they mature and take on more responsibility. It is important for parents to strike a balance between giving their child more privacy and continuing to show an interest in their friends and activities. Teenagers tend to test the limits of boundaries as they move toward adulthood, so negotiation, communication and patience is necessary to assist their development during this stage. As with every stage of development, enjoyment, freedom, fun, unconditional love and nurturing is vital to the creation and maintenance of a child's healthy self-esteem and solid boundaries.

Even parents with the best of intentions find teaching healthy and appropriate boundaries to be an extremely difficult balancing act. After reading about the five stages of development, you may realize not all of your childhood needs were met. There is almost certainly not a person alive that could have understood and met every one of our needs. No wonder so many people lack a healthy concept of "self" and boundaries! Most of us would probably greatly benefit from healing work in this area.

As with every aspect of the healing process, change starts with awareness. Like many people, I had no idea I had issues regarding boundaries. After repeated experiences of disrespect and pain, I eventually hit rock bottom and had to face the truth—I had boundary issues! I started to understand I was lacking a solid internal sense of self. I needed to focus on this in order to heal. An entry point or a trigger (which usually includes disillusionment or pain) is often needed to shake up our old belief systems so we will open to change. This is what happened to me.

As I embarked on my healing journey, I started to realize that boundaries in my family of origin were pretty much nonexistent. Some family members would shirk responsibility, while others would try to balance things out by taking on more than their fair share.

As with many families, expressing certain emotions was not acceptable—especially anger. There was only one person allowed to express anger in my family and that was my stepfather. I learned at an early age that I should not speak up if I was upset or disagreed with someone. I was not even allowed to express my own opinion. I learned that "playing opossum" was my most effective survival technique. While my stepfather would rage, the rest of us kept quiet and did our best not to rock the boat. We became little People Pleasers.

Children often take on the responsibility of appeasing other family members. They attempt to take care of their parents' sadness or anger, hoping they can fix things and make them better. In order to keep peace, I learned to be quiet and began to believe others were more important than me. Essentially, I learned to hide my truth. These were not conscious choices. I was simply doing what I needed to do for the sake of acceptance and survival.

This is a common childhood experience and is usually carried over into adulthood. These patterns repeat themselves until things get so bad that we eventually realize things have to be different.

It is critical we recognize our need for healthy boundaries in order to start creating them. The first step in the process is to realize we deserve honor and respect so we can convey this to others. It is important to feel our emotions, to know we have the right to articulate what is true for us and to speak up on our own behalf. We must learn how to be honest with ourselves and with others. If we do not awaken to this belief and understanding, we will continue to manifest unhealthy relationships. If we do not take responsibility for our boundaries, there will always be someone stepping over them. Without healthy boundaries, we will continually be hurt, exploited and victimized.

It is easier to set boundaries with people we care little about. Setting boundaries in the relationships that mean the most to us can be more challenging. Especially when we think we want or need someone in our lives and desire their approval. This is the area of our Inner Child's deepest wounds. Healing our Inner Child can be an important part of establishing boundaries.

Recovering or establishing boundaries you have never had can be difficult and often painful. However, it is essential if you ever want to feel safe in the world and manifest healthy, supportive and truly loving relationships. It is important to realize that you matter - you are important! You have the right to be happy, protected and respected. In fact, a profound shift occurs when you realize *you need to be the most important person in your life!*

Some people may think this is selfish. However, it is only from this place of loving our Self that we have the capacity to share the best parts of ourselves with others. When we love ourselves and are cognizant of our boundaries, we are able to share from a full well. It is a huge shift to go from being "other-oriented" to becoming "self-oriented," and from seeking approval outside of oneself to living in a place of self-approval.

To be in a solid healthy relationship with someone else, we have to create a solid relationship with ourselves. I remember a teacher once telling me that in a healthy partnership, we make Spirit first, ourself second and our partner third. I had never considered this before and, at the time, it seemed unromantic and selfish. However, I now know from my own experience that this wisdom is profound and true.

There is a romantic notion about connecting, bonding and relating to another person, especially in committed love relationships. It goes something like this: You make your lover's needs your priority and they make your needs their priority. Both of your needs are met by each other all the time! It's a nice sentiment, but it never seems to work well for very long.

It is unrealistic to think someone is going to give you everything you want and need exactly when you want and need it. Believing this sets you up for inevitable disappointment, frustration and pain. There is no getting around it, successful relationships are built on the solid foundation that exists within each partner. In my opinion, being diligent and clear with personal boundaries is more essential in our romantic partnerships than anywhere else.

Michael and Sharon

Michael and Sharon are a couple with healthy boundaries. When they are at the movies and Michael is not enjoying the film, he tells Sharon he will step out and reconnect with her after it is over. The first time Michael did this, Sharon felt a little confused and disappointed. Michael explained that he was not enjoying the movie and was speaking up on his own behalf. He was making a choice that he was comfortable with and honoring himself. After discussing it, Sharon understood and agreed that Michael should take care of his own needs, while allowing her the opportunity to make her self-honoring choice to finish watching the movie. In this case, both Michael and Sharon are being true to themselves, mindful of their personal boundaries and making self-honoring choices.

When we speak up honestly and honor ourselves, we are taking responsibility for our own experiences and our own lives. We are not handing over the responsibility of our happiness to someone else. We are clear where we begin and end. We also respect and value the differences between ourselves and others.

Exercise: Strengthening Our Boundaries

An essential step in successfully defining and expressing boundaries is the ability to communicate without blaming. We need to be able to take responsibility for our feelings. Rather than saying, "You make me angry" or "You make me sad," a more responsible way of articulating your emotions would be "I am feeling angry" or "I am feeling sad." A formula for emotionally honest communication and establishing healthy boundaries would look something like this:

- When you…

- I feel…

- I would appreciate…

- And what I will do for myself is…

- I have no control over you and am speaking up on my behalf. I am asking for what I want and will take the action steps necessary to make myself feel better.

Example:

When you do not pick up after yourself or do the dishes,

I feel upset and frustrated. I feel you do not respect me.

I would appreciate you cleaning up after yourself and washing the dishes.

I have no control over you and am speaking up on my behalf. I am asking for what I want and will take the action steps necessary to make myself feel better.

In this example, the partner may or may not respond favorably to the other person speaking their truth. If they do not respond favorably, other supportive actions steps may need to be implemented. We do not have control over others, so consider what *is* in your control and what *you can do* to make yourself feel better.

Example: Supportive Action Steps

Setting up a weekly chore schedule.

Hiring a housekeeper come every week or two for support and assistance.

Use this formula for articulating your truth, expressing your feelings and accepting personal responsibility. This will help you to take care of yourself and effectively set healthy personal boundaries.

Exercise: Creating Healthy Boundaries

Take a few minutes to reflect and write about an area of your life where you feel someone has been infringing on your boundaries or where you are not being completely respected. What is this person doing and how are you feeling?

1. One key to recognizing this is to look for any resentment you may be experiencing. When you have identified such a situation, finish the following sentence.

When you...

2. Explore and express how this "infringement" makes you feel.

I feel...

3. Articulate what you would appreciate as an alternative. Be specific.

I would appreciate...

4. Acknowledge your lack of control over the other person and take personal responsibility.

I have no control over you, I am speaking up on my behalf, asking for what I want and will take the action steps necessary to make myself feel better.

5. Consider and write down action steps you can take to support and honor yourself. Be specific.

Boundaries require honest and direct communication. Although creating them can be challenging, they are necessary to respect, love, protect and care for ourselves and to connect more fully and deeply with others. When we learn how to set boundaries, we more effectively define our territory and protect our "space" physically, financially, mentally, emotionally and spiritually. Setting and maintaining boundaries protects our personal connection to Spirit and supports us in making that connection a priority. Our boundaries assist us in aligning with our Higher Self, our authentic power and in living up to our fullest potential. Ultimately, strong boundaries create a powerful sense of freedom and safety within ourselves and in all of our relationships.

Chapter 12
Receiving and Giving

Giving and receiving are like breathing, both inhaling and exhaling are necessary for a balanced, healthy life.
~ Tammi Baliszewski

To the bee a flower is a fountain of life, and to the flower a bee is a messenger of love. And to both bee and flower, giving and receiving is a need and an ecstasy.
~ Kahlil Gibran

Most of us are familiar with the phrase, "It is better to give than to receive." As children, we were taught to give; however, many of us were not taught how to receive. Generously giving and graciously receiving are equally important and vital to manifesting and maintaining a balanced, healthy relationship.

Based on my personal experiences and those of my clients, I find many people have difficulty when it comes to receiving. They tend to have a belief system based on unworthiness and scarcity. They feel a need to "get" or "grab" things outside of themselves. Those with truly abundant and loving lives "let" rather than "get." They "allow" rather than "chase." If you do not have all that you want, need and desire in your life, you probably have a challenge with receiving.

How well do you receive? Do you dismiss or deflect compliments? Do you feel obligated to return them or do you graciously and joyfully receive compliments? How do you respond when someone says, "You look great in that outfit!"? Do you say:

"Oh no!" or "oh, yuck!" (Dismissed)

"Yeah, if I could lose 10 pounds!" or "Gee, I thought I looked fat!" (Disregarded)

"I've had this old thing for years." or "I bought it at a garage sale for two dollars." (Diminished)

"Gross!" or "Absolutely not!" (Rejected)

"Oh no, your outfit is great!" (Deflected)

"Oh, why thank you very much!" or "I really appreciate you noticing!" (Graciously and joyfully received!)

Receiving graciously and joyfully is more than just a perfunctory "thanks." It is allowing the compliment, gift or act of kindness into your heart. It is taking the time and energy to acknowledge the person who is extending the kindness. It is also acknowledging and receiving the love behind their actions and words.

Many of us find it more difficult to receive than to give. Here are a few possible reasons why some of us might feel the way we do:

We feel an internal lack of personal value and self worth

We feel out of control, overwhelmed, vulnerable or weak

We feel indebted or that we will owe the person who gives to us

We believe it is better to give than to receive.

It feels unfamiliar, embarrassing or uncomfortable

We want to appear humble

We do not want to be perceived as greedy or selfish

We desire to appear independent, self-sufficient and self-reliant

If a person cannot receive graciously and joyfully, they tend to end up in relationships with "takers." Depletion, depression and exhaustion will follow. Over the years, I have observed many women in relationships with successful men. When the relationships end, many of these women ended up with less energy, less money and a diminished sense of value. They often ask, "How did this happen to me?" My response is, "You did not believe in your own value. You got exactly what you believed you deserved."

Some of these women have a superficial sense of worth. They do their hair and makeup and know, on the surface, they look pretty good. One woman described her actions as putting frosting on a cardboard box to make it look like a beautiful cake. However, deep down inside, she did not feel good about herself, value herself or believe in her substance.

A sense of having no value or worth was a familiar feeling in my life. After the breakup with my fiancé Bob, I came out of the relationship with less money than I had going into it. He was a very successful man and made millions of dollars every year. At the beginning of the engagement, I was advised by our therapist to give up my job so I could emotionally support him full time. According to our therapist, being his fiancé was now my "job." I did as I was told and for three years I put my life on hold to take care of him. When the relationship ended, I was told to go away.

I could not believe it! I felt I should get something for making this man, his career and his life my priority. When I mentioned this to him, he informed me that I deserved nothing. When I meditated, I asked "Why am I taken advantage of? Why I am I always abandoned and left with nothing?" The answer was simple. I got what I believed I was worth—nothing. If I could not even accept a simple compliment or lunch from a good friend, how could I expect to receive great love, abundance and all the riches of the universe?

I must admit I was far from being a gracious receiver in many ways. At Christmas one year, Bob gave me a pair of eight-carat diamond earrings. My response to his generous gift was, "Why are you wasting your money on me?" I did not believe I deserved them.

All of us manifest exactly what we believe we are worth. I finally began to understand some of my lessons that were coming out of this heartbreaking relationship. I needed to start working on my issues of self worth. I needed to learn how to say "thank you" without argument, shutting down and pushing kindness away.

A friend once said to me, "Tammi, when you do not receive, you are not allowing the person who wants to enjoy the experience of giving." I now understand by not joyfully and graciously receiving, I not only reject the gift, I reject the heart and the energy of the person who wants to share with me.

If we do not receive well, we will end up feeling depleted and empty. Energetically, non-receivers emit a vibration of lack and deficit. When a person feels deficient, they need to replenish themselves in some way. They often become "energy vampires."

At the other end of the spectrum are gold diggers. They are people who "grab" and have the greedy vibration of a taker and user. This also stems from a belief in lack and scarcity. Gold diggers are narcissists and have a sense of entitlement. They too have deep-seated issues regarding self worth. In an attempt to validate and substantiate their value, they feel a need to fill up using people and things from outside of themselves.

Some people hesitate to ask for what they want and do not receive joyfully and graciously. Some people feel entitled, grab at all they can get thinking only of themselves and believe other people owe them. Others try to get more than they believe they deserve to compensate for an internal sense of worthlessness and powerlessness. All of these types of people can benefit enormously from cultivating an authentic loving relationship with themselves and learning to receive graciously.

Ultimately, the receiving process needs to begin from within. Before we can fully appreciate and receive someone else's generosity, we must be able to give generously to ourselves. We need to be able to nurture ourselves with respect and compassion. We need to honor our hunger, fatigue, feelings and truth. Until we do, it will be impossible for someone or something outside of ourselves to give us what we truly want. It is necessary to care for ourselves and feel deserving before we can graciously receive compliments, respect or love from someone else.

When I worked as a massage therapist, the most exhausting clients were "givers" who were unable to relax and receive. I felt frustrated and depleted at the end of these sessions because of their resistance—it was like trying to push an elephant through a keyhole. While I understood receiving is difficult for some people due to issues with guilt or unworthiness, it made my job much harder. On the other hand, when a client was able to relax and receive, their gratitude made me feel appreciated and energized. It felt as if a cycle of energy was present; a graceful flow of giving and receiving and a wonderfully balanced exchange.

While meditating on the dynamics of giving, taking and receiving, two scenarios came to mind. First, I envisioned a child at Christmas. Excited about her presents, she quickly rips each gift open without any acknowledgement and hastily moves on to the next. When the last of the presents have been torn open and discarded, she expresses her disappointment that the experience is over. She is upset with the quantity of gifts she received and that she did not get *everything* she wanted. In the second situation, another little girl is just as excited. She is present "in the moment" and expresses heartfelt appreciation for each gift and for the overall experience. In which situation, and with which child, do you think the parents would want to do more for in the future?

I have wondered if God sees many of us as impatient and ungrateful children, whining about things not being different or better and asking why we cannot have more. We rip through the gifts of the world that are so generously bestowed on us, all the while complaining. Many of us focus on what we *do not* have rather than what we *do* have. We often complain rather than appreciate. I have put forth conscious effort and made great strides with being appreciative and graciously receiving. Gratitude has been a powerful catalyst to opening the floodgates of profound abundance, love, miracles and support in all areas of my life.

While my husband and I were still dating, there was a time when I experienced great discomfort. Initially, I could not understand why. I finally realized it was overwhelming and foreign for me to "sit" in this much loving—I felt I had hit my upper limits. I said I wanted a relationship with a loving man and had certainly done a great deal of inner work to get to this place. Now that I had manifested it, I was not sure what to do with it! When I meditated about my confusion and discomfort, I realized I just needed to relax, allow and receive.

Expanding and allowing more love in can take some getting used to. Receiving love can be like stretching your body when your muscles are tight. You have to go slow, be patient and keep stretching.

One day while meditating, I envisioned a funnel. I noticed that the narrow end of the funnel is constricted and does not allow much to flow through. Similarly, if we are constricted within ourselves and do not believe in our value, we cannot allow good to come into our lives. Everything we manifest has to do with our internal sense of worthiness and our connection to Spirit. We need to be able to breathe and graciously receive love and support from God, in order to attract and receive the gifts and wonders of the world.

Giving and receiving are both wonderful blessings. As you learn to receive graciously, you will find it is easy and natural to give generously. When we are fulfilled and abundant, we have so much more to share. Only when we are balanced in our ability to give and receive will we be able to experience the miracles and generosity of the universe.

The art of gracious receiving is a skill, social grace and a powerful gift. As with all skills, we get better with practice. Set an intention to receive graciously and joyfully. The next time someone gives you a compliment, offers assistance or a gesture of kindness; pay attention to them, graciously and joyfully receive. As we become conscious of the power of receiving, interacting with others becomes more authentic, heartfelt and enjoyable. By graciously receiving, we acknowledge, validate and appreciate the one who wants to give. Both the giver and the receiver benefit!

If you do not have all you desire, examine your internal constrictions. To experience life from a place of appreciation and reverence opens us to miracles and prosperity. Gratitude expands our hearts and creates a magnetic attraction that draws to us unforeseen blessings, profound joy and great love.

Exercise: Expansive Receiving and Giving

1. Take a moment to remember the most favorite gift you ever received. Take the time to recall this experience as vividly as possible. Allow yourself to experience the expansive feeling of receiving—delight in the thrill, deliciousness and excitement. Bask in and allow these feelings to expand. Then let the energy of gratitude and appreciation fill you completely. Write about your experience in your journal.

2. Now try to remember a special gift you gave to a loved one. Recall the experience. Bask in the positive feelings of giving from the heart. Now let the energy of giving fill you completely for as long as you can. Write about your experience in your journal.

3. Go within yourself, relax and take a few deep cleansing breaths. With your eyes closed, ask yourself these questions: *What do I want to receive right now? What is my heart's desire?*

   Write the answer in your journal.

4. What was your answer? Love? Jewelry? A new car? Think about how you can provide this for yourself right now. If your desire is a new car (or something that is not in your current budget), look for something symbolic, such as a model car. If more love is your desire, find and wear a simple heart pendant or find a symbol to place in your home. This is a clear, powerful and tangible way to let the universe know what you want. This powerful magnet anchors your focus, energy and intention to manifest your heart's desire.

5. Experiencing and expressing sincere gratitude is the most important way to open more fully to receiving. Take a few minutes to review your life and capture in writing those qualities, experiences and possessions you hold most precious. This list could include gratitude for your health, family, friends, abundance and talents you possess.

6. Take a few moments to thank Spirit for the beauty of the world, the gift of life and for everything you appreciate.

When we focus our thoughts and energy toward the things we are grateful for, we soften and release constrictions that prevent us from being able to receive opportunities, assistance, abundance and love. Review this list or create a new list daily or weekly. Get ready to receive wonderful gifts and blessings from the universe!

Exercise: Visualization

You may read through this exercise and do it by memory, have someone read it aloud to you, or make a recording of it in your own voice. Go slowly and give yourself the opportunity to really visualize and feel this process. (If you have a heart condition, check with your physician before attempting to do this).

Close your eyes and focus your attention on your heart. Feel its energy, feel it beating and express gratitude for its magnificence. Imagine the energy of your heart starting to grow and expand like a flower coming into full bloom or a ball of sunshine growing within you. You are now opening and expanding your heart to receive God's love. Imagine your heart gently and graciously opening, receiving more wonderful experiences, incredible gifts, divinely inspired ideas and relationships. Allow yourself to feel a deep sense of gratitude and appreciation. Imagine this energy of gratitude filling your whole body. Now allow it to expand it out to your community, the nation, the earth and the entire universe. Sit in this place of connection, joy and gratitude for as long as you desire.

The greatest gift we will ever know is to love and be loved in return. In every encounter we have the opportunity to give others the love, respect and compassion we wish to receive. As we do this, we can touch and heal the hearts of others and, in turn, our own. Our energy and existence in this world creates a ripple effect. The ripple effect of love is the most powerful and most healing of all. When you choose to step more fully into your love, not only does it serve you, it blesses all of humanity.

Chapter 13
Manipulation versus Authentic Power

Where love rules there is no will to power and where power predominates love is lacking. One is the shadow of the other.
~ Carl Jung

There is a big difference between the love of power and the power of love.
~ Anonymous

Most of us go through a good portion of our lives semiconscious or unconscious of our true needs and desires. We often learn about fear, doubt and lack from our parents and through our life experiences. Many of us question who we are as well as our ability to create the life of our dreams. Most people believe they have to look outside of themselves for the things they need to feel happy and fulfilled. Inevitably, if we do not realize we have the power of the universe within us, we will attempt to attach ourselves to others who will care for us in ways we cannot or will not care for ourselves.

All of us are born with an internal guidance system made up of our emotions and intuition. However, if our guidance system is ignored, it will eventually become a dull whisper then seemingly silent. If you observe babies, you find they know what they want and when they want it. They cry if they are hungry or need changing; they laugh if they feel happy and joyful; and they sleep if they are tired. Babies live in the present moment. They are attuned and living in alignment with their internal guidance systems.

The disconnection from our guidance system begins when our parents, family, friends, teachers and society tell us certain feelings and behaviors are wrong, bad or inappropriate. Issues of self-worth start to arise. As time goes on, it becomes less clear to us what we want and need. We often lose touch with the desire to create, tell the truth, express our feelings and play. Our feelings can become stifled, distorted or blown out of proportion.

Some of us are unfulfilled in ways we cannot even identify. Many of us have a yearning deep inside, but we cannot explain what it is. We distract and attempt to soothe ourselves by focusing on external things we believe will make us feel better—a bigger house, a different job, a new car, shopping, food or finding that "perfect" relationship.

Dependency is perhaps one of the most common personality disorders. If we do not understand the magnitude of our personal power and consciously connect with it, we will constantly seek to attach ourselves to those we perceive as having more or different power than we do.

As mentioned in a previous chapter, the desire to manifest a relationship in order to fill a perceived void always leads to disappointment. When we believe there is something wrong or missing within us, we often attempt to attach ourselves to someone else in order to give us a sense of value, worth, purpose and direction. We may then, consciously or unconsciously, start to live for them. When we hand over our power to a source outside of ourselves, we become psychologically and emotionally dependent.

The energetic or unspoken dialogue within this dynamic may be "I love you, but you have to love me the way I want you to." Some people may even extend this dialogue with "—or else!" I have seen and personally experienced many relationships where there has been destructive, manipulative and vindictive behavior—all in the name of love. More accurate terms for this type of connection would be *co-dependency, emotional blackmail* or *manipulation*. This type of relationship is based on expectations, conditions and requirements, and if they are not met, "there will be hell to pay!" Resentment, frustration, anger and even hatred can result. The saying, "There is a thin line between love and hate" accurately fits this type of relationship.

In order to manifest a truly healthy relationship, you must be consciously connected to your internal source of power. If not, you will feel out of control, fearful, manipulated and most likely angry. After all, it is scary to feel as if you have no personal power in your own life. In emotionally dependent relationships, there will inevitably be power plays and control dramas as each person struggles to take control of their own experience.

Control Dramas

There are two primary ways to control others, either overtly or covertly. An example of an overt control drama involves the *"aggressor"* and the *"interrogator."* A covert control drama involves the *"victim"* and the *"passive aggressor."* Each of the players in these control dramas has specific character traits.

Aggressor. Aggressors are overbearing people that will do anything to get what they want. They tend to be loud, threatening and possibly prone to violence. They are bullies and try to manipulate and control out of a sense of their own powerlessness. Their motto would be something like, "It's better to be the kicker than the kickee."

Interrogator. Interrogators are people who probe and ask questions in a critical or condescending manner. They tend to be demeaning and constantly finding fault. For example, interrogators might say, "Do you think it was smart to knock over the glass of milk?," "Do you think it's okay to be wasteful and disrespectful?," or "Are you clumsy or just stupid?" They often use their intellect as a way of proving their superiority.

Victim. Victims perceive themselves as innocent scapegoats. Their self-image is that of a martyr who is always being attacked by aggressors and predators. They are the downtrodden, the abused and the "poor me" type. Guilt is a tactic often used by victims in an attempt to have some sense of power or control over others so they can get what they want.

Passive-Aggressor. Passive-aggressors are known for giving you the silent treatment or simply saying, "whatever!" before they turn on their heels and walk away. They are aloof, sullen and may pout. They like to create an air of mystery and intrigue so people will come after them, thus having a shallow sense of power or control.

All of these behaviors are ways that people try to overpower or even suck the power from those around them. They devalue others in order to elevate themselves. This provides them with temporary relief from their sense of disempowerment. People use control dramas and manipulation because they feel inferior or a void inside themselves. They believe power, control, wholeness, happiness and love can be obtained from the world outside of themselves. All forms of control and manipulation stem from the ego: feeling competitive with, separate from, superior or inferior to others.

Although these tactics may be successful in the short term, attempting to control and manipulate others is only a temporary fix. This behavior will never truly fill the sense of emptiness. It is similar to putting a small bandage over an infected wound that will not heal. Control dramas and manipulation prevent people from experiencing Authentic Power, connection, intimacy and unconditional love. Unless they become aware of their manipulative behavior and work to overcome it, they will never be able to create the environment necessary for loving, supportive, committed and soul-expanding relationships.

Authentic Power

There is a monumental difference between power with a lower case *p* and power with a capital *P*. Authentic Power comes from within. It is an awareness of Self and knowing that all you need will be provided by Spirit. When you consciously align with this Power, you will not be prone to manipulate others. Regardless of anyone else's behavior, you know that you are connected to God, the only true Power and therefore completely whole unto yourself.

We all learned how to get attention early in life, typically from our family. Often, we continue to use the same tactics in subsequent relationships. In order to come into Authentic Power, it is helpful to review our personal history. We can become aware of our control dramas and manipulative tendencies by looking back at our childhood. Ask yourself which member of your family had the most power. How did they get the power and how did they keep it? How did you protect yourself, obtain power and get your needs met?

Once we understand our learned perceptions of power and how we attempted to get our needs met as children, we can focus on fully recognizing, cultivating and claiming our Authentic Power.

As a child, I was not allowed to express anger. I learned the only way to get attention was to pout or to be passive aggressive. As an adult, I continued to use this immature behavior in order to gain control and power in my relationships. When I was upset with Bob, I would often give him the silent treatment. I would often say, "Whatever!" Or go home and not answer the phone when he called. He would often become frantic in his efforts to contact me. A part of me liked knowing he cared enough to come after me—until one day he did not.

My manipulation definitely contributed to the demise of the relationship. Control and manipulation seemed effective in getting me what I wanted in the short term. However, it caused considerable damage to the relationship over the long term.

To move from an immature, outwardly dependant relationship to a mature, healthy, authentically loving relationship, you must first realize true Power resides within. When you pull your energy back, align with Spirit and live from your center, you are more capable of communicating from a connected, stable and honest place. Ultimately, your source of Power comes from the same energy that breathes you. In other words, the only Authentic Power is spiritual power.

As with so many things, change and healing begins with awareness and intention. When you start to feel frustrated with someone else, it helps to remember that you are whole unto yourself. In the end, I believe all challenges are really about your relationship with yourself and your connection to Spirit.

When people live from the empowered place within, rather than using a control drama to get what they want, they simply tell their truth (Chapter 11 on boundaries gave a good example of this). One way of stating your truth is by getting in touch with your feelings and your bodily sensations and then sharing your experience from a physical perspective.

Examples of communicating from the place of Authentic Power:

When you yell at me, I feel a knot in my stomach. I would like to continue to communicate, but if you continue to yell, we will have this conversation later when we are both calm.

As you are making the suggestion for us to connect with your friends on Saturday, my head is starting to hurt. I would like to take some time to understand what this is about before we commit to anything.

When you changed our plans at the last minute, I felt dismissed and unimportant. In the future, I would appreciate being included in the decision-making process.

Honest communication can be challenging. In the heat of the moment when there is anger, hurt and frustration, there can be confusion. It is good to remember taking time for ourselves can help us to find balance, clarity and to become centered again.

Meditation is a great way to anchor ourselves, get back to our center and cultivate our spiritual power. Just like a cell phone needs to be plugged in to recharge its battery, we need to consciously replenish and realign ourselves to become integrated and clear.

Our minds are the place where fear is created. During meditation, we are giving our "thinking minds" a break, so the energy of our heart and soul can bubble up. As human beings, our essence is one of love, peace and joy. By relaxing our minds and slowing down the constant barrage of thoughts, we align with that essence.

Finding my own Authentic Power has been an incredible experience. Occasionally, I become amused when I see that I am reverting back to manipulation with my "old friends" the passive aggressor and the victim. One time I wanted something from Steve and he did not comply. He asked me if I was starting to pout. I said, "Yes! Because I'm five and I want things my way!" Steve reminded me of my connection to Spirit and my Authentic Power. I laughed and surrendered the pout.

Humor is a great quality to have while making the transition from an old way of behaving to a new one. It is wonderful to have support from those who know us well and can point out when we are up to our old tricks.

Authentic Power comes from the awareness that we are a part of something much greater than ourselves. This "something greater" is on our side, moving through us, directing us, encouraging us and loving us. From this place of connection we are aligned, whole, confident and joyful. When we are genuinely empowered, we are free to be who we truly are—whole and divine. We know all of our needs will be met and our True Power comes from within and beyond.

Exercise: Cultivating Authentic Power

1. Review the players in control dramas—the aggressor, interrogator, victim and passive aggressor. In writing, describe the roles you tend to use.

2. Write down an example of when you used this manipulative tactic in your recent past. Describe what happened outwardly and inwardly during this situation.

3. Using your example, describe how you could have responded from your place of Authentic Power (that is, more loving, compassionate, etc.).

4. Take a moment to visualize and imagine fully stepping into the experience of Authentic Power. What does it feel like? How are things different? What does life look like from this perspective?

Additional Empowering Principles

Authentic Power occurs naturally when you:
Do your best to find your internal spiritual focal point and cultivate your personal connection with God.

Are willing to be 100 percent responsible for your thoughts, actions and reactions.

Choose to live your life in a way that exemplifies integrity and honor.

Learn to communicate from your heart and speak your truth.

Are willing to participate whole-heartedly and honestly in life and relationships while surrendering any attachment to the outcome.

Strive for harmony, balance, cooperation and sharing.

Live in a place of gratitude and reverence.

Affirm and maintain the awareness that there is no competition, only connection.

Realize everything you need comes from your connection to Spirit within.

Chapter 14
Balancing the Masculine and Feminine

This is not a gender issue, it is an issue of
how best to develop a fully integrated consciousness
as the foundation for effective relationship...
honoring both the male and female energies within all of us.
~ Gavin Frye

Each of us has an anima and animus, the masculine
and feminine counterpart within us. The integration of these
aspects is essential on the path to individuation and wholeness.
~ Carl Jung

There are hundreds, maybe thousands, of books available about dating, relationships and finding love. Many of them tell us how different we are as men and women. Some would even have us believe we are from different parts of the universe! Often these books provide advice on how to behave, what to say and what to do (or not do) in order to get what you want from a romantic partner. I have read many of these books and have actually found some of them valuable.

Although there can be significant differences in behavior, communication styles and the desires of men and women, the essence of who we are is not so very different. At the core, I believe we have the same essential needs—to be seen, heard, appreciated, respected, cared for and loved. We are *all* thinking, feeling and creative beings.

Carl Jung believed the psyche to be androgynous. Our souls are made up of both masculine and feminine (or yin and yang) qualities. When I speak of the "feminine" this does not pertain just to women and the "masculine" does not pertain only to men. These are inner psychological characteristics and traits we all possess. No person is completely masculine or completely feminine. Masculine and feminine energies are innate and essential qualities that are a part of each and every one of us. Our individual and collective experience of balance and wholeness requires a synthesis of our primary traits with their complementary opposites.

Feminine energy is oriented inward. Loving, listening and relating to others are considered to be a feminine qualities. It is in our receiving (a feminine attribute) that we feel and relate. Masculine energy is oriented outward. It is the ability to control situations and defend our territory. It is what motivates us to take action. When we are truly receptive (feminine) and aligned with Spirit we can take clear effective action (masculine) in the world. When this balance is achieved, we can experience and express our Authentic Power. To become a healthy, whole and empowered man or woman, each of us needs to develop and implement our complimentary natures. We need to be able to love and take action; we need to think as well as feel.

From my perspective, the world is out of balance—it is extremely masculine. Masculine qualities, such as the accumulation of wealth, taking action and possessing strength, are revered and perceived as superior by most. These are the energies of doing, getting and having. Constant competition, the overwhelming need for personal power and the desire to rule the world, leaves little room for introspection, gratitude and connection.

The feminine energy is devalued, suppressed and disregarded by much of the world. Without feminine qualities, we are led in the direction of aggression, famine, competition, destruction, cruelty and chaos.

I am not implying that men are bad, or that masculine qualities are not valuable and important. Masculine energy *is* important, vital, necessary and essential for each of us as individuals and for the good of the world. Without masculine qualities, we lose focus, ambition and motivation. We are not grounded or productive.

Power to take action (masculine) without love and compassion (feminine) becomes brutality. Emotion (feminine) without motivation and initiative (masculine) becomes sappy and overly sentimental.

Historians discovered God was depicted as female long before She was portrayed as male. Dating back thousands of years before Christ, art and figurines were found that honored the Divine Feminine. However, we do not see or hear much about Her in our modern religious teachings. It is time for us to acknowledge both the Divine Feminine and the Divine Masculine. Any fragmentation, suppression or denial of the Divine Feminine or Masculine, will lead to imbalance in the world.

When one side of our nature is repressed it will become a disowned aspect of ourselves and create an imbalance. Sometimes it is necessary to experience being out of balance to realize we need to make changes.

It is the universe's intention that we become whole complete. Human nature will not tolerate imbalance indefinitely. Attempts at balance and wholeness usually begin with discord and conflict. If we ignore the "hints," our disowned nature will become more powerful and make itself known to us one way or another. Imbalance can show up in the form of tragedy, chaos, loss, conflict, neurosis, obsessions, addiction, illness, accidents or depression.

In order to cultivate wholeness, we need to combine our masculine and feminine qualities. When we acknowledge and implement these traits, we become whole personally and collectively. This strengthens the foundation for healthy loving relationships.

The following is a partial list of masculine and feminine qualities:

Masculine	Feminine
Goal oriented	*Feeling oriented*
Determined	*Nurturing*
Logical	*Emotional*
Analytical	*Intuitive*
Controlling	*Receptive*
Rational	*Creative*
Competitive	*Cooperative*
Physical	*Compassionate*
Externally focused	*Internally focused*
Powerful	*Empowering*
Independent	*Family-oriented*
Proactive	*Passive*
Self-contained	*Inclusive*

When either masculine or feminine traits are out of balance (or denied) our whole being suffers. Awareness is the first key to balance. When we become aware of the qualities we need to embrace and embody, we can make a conscious choice to cultivate and integrate these traits.

In the past, I buried and denied many of both my feminine and masculine qualities. Even though I consider myself very feminine, I had deep-seated judgments about myself and my femininity. Many of my women clients have similar judgments of inferiority and shame.

Many men have judgments about accepting and integrating feminine qualities and often struggle to express them. A side effect of the denial of these traits can be a "need" to be in a relationship, a tendency to objectify women, conquer women and love-hate relationships. When a man cannot access the feminine within himself, he will be on the prowl seeking the embodiment of the "feminine" from someone outside of himself. This is a dysfunctional (and usually unconscious) attempt at integration and wholeness.

I often hear men and women fighting. They argue, criticize, find fault and demean each other in an attempt to win arguments. This behavior flows from an imbalance of traits. The desire to compete and win is a masculine tendency. The desire to listen and deeply understand is feminine in nature. To build and sustain a healthy and whole relationship, its foundation must be built on both masculine and feminine qualities. However, the feminine qualities of listening, appreciation and compassion are vital to communication, especially during times of conflict and misunderstanding. I believe if more people truly listened with the intent to understand another, rather than "win," there would be far more successful and happy long-term partnerships.

There comes a time in many relationships when thinking and reasoning do not give us the answers we need. We simply cannot figure out life or what to do about our problems. This is when we need to surrender to the qualities of the feminine and to the unconscious. One of the great strengths of the feminine is to simply be - be still, relax, be patient and go with the natural ebb and flow of the universe. This means we surrender to God. Optimal balance occurs from partnering with Spirit, being patient and allowing clarity to come forth (qualities of the feminine) and, once we have clarity, stepping up, taking action, being proactive and diligent (qualities of the masculine).

The evolution of our soul occurs when we become aware of our disowned or conflicting aspects and by welcoming, embracing and integrating them. By taking personal responsibility and developing our less-developed traits, we become whole. This is an incredibly powerful step in our personal healing. It is also important for the healing and evolution of the planet.

If you consider the state of the world, you may feel change is needed. From this chaotic state, many of us will set a personal intention for balance, healing and wholeness. It is through seeking and finding our wholeness that we will experience connection and harmony in our careers, our health, in our love relationships and in the world.

Taking the journey inward takes courage, commitment, faith and fortitude. We all have the ability to succeed. The choice to take this journey is not an option. The option you *do* have is whether you take it now or later. When we choose to embark on this journey we are met by angels, seen and unseen, to support us along the way.

Exercise: Balancing the Masculine and the Feminine

1. Review the list of masculine and feminine qualities. Write down the qualities that you believe you embody.

2. List the qualities you feel you are lacking, suppressing, or ignoring.

3. Now ask your intuition to share with you which qualities could you benefit the most from cultivating, integrating, or owning and write them down.

4. After becoming aware of the qualities that need the most attention, go within and ask, *"What can I do to bring*

myself more fully into my ideal state of wholeness and balance?" Write down your answers.

5. Create a list of action steps that you can take now, to bring yourself into optimal balance.

6. Take a few moments to imagine and write down how it will *feel* to fully accept, integrate and embrace your personal wholeness. What is it like to stand in your full power? How are you treated? How is life different?

7. Write down any additional revelations or lessons that have surfaced through this process.

Chapter 15
Intimacy

Games are a compromise between intimacy and
keeping intimacy away.
~Eric Berne

It boils down to this: Are you willing to have your relationships
be a pathway to fully revealing yourself and your potential?
If your answer is yes, real intimacy can
be yours on a daily basis.
~ Gay Hendricks

Intimacy is both the ability and the choice to be close, loving and vulnerable. It requires identity development; you have to know yourself, love yourself and maintain healthy boundaries in order to cultivate true intimacy. These qualities are vital so you do not overpower your partner or lose your sense of self in the relationship. The word intimacy is often used to imply a sexual experience; however, it is possible to have a sexual encounter without intimacy, as well as intimacy without having sex.

True intimacy begins within ourselves and extends outward. A level of self-trust, self-understanding and an innate sense of value is necessary before we can share ourselves honestly with someone else. We must feel who we are is good in order to allow ourselves to be truly seen - *"in-to-me-see"*.

Intimacy is the capacity and the desire to allow another human being to experience our very essence.

Intimacy occurs when we lower our emotional masks and connect from an authentic place. It requires the ability and desire to share ourselves without hiding, editing, controlling or manipulating. Intimate relationships allow you to reveal yourself as you truly are.

Although most of us desire intimacy, we fear it at the same time. Unresolved pain from our childhood or past relationships can prevent us from lowering our walls of protection. Very few people reach adulthood unscathed. The walls that seemingly protect us also prevent us from connecting deeply with others.

Our training for intimate relationships begins early. Some of the childhood experiences that can create challenges with intimacy later on include:

Not having enough space or freedom early in life.

Having too much space and not enough structure, discipline or boundaries.

Not having enough physical contact or affection.

Being touched inappropriately.

Being abused.

Being betrayed or abandoned.

Not being allowed to express feelings.

Not being allowed or encouraged to be yourself.

Having harsh, angry or abusive parents or caretakers.

Having a parent who neglected you or was absent.

Having parents who were alcoholics or addicts of any kind.

Having parents who were not parented well themselves and looked to you to fulfill their needs.

Experiencing significant trauma such as divorce, death or health problems.

As children, if we were not allowed and encouraged to be authentic, intimacy and genuine heartfelt connections will be more difficult as an adult. We learn to cover up our fears and deny our feelings in order to be accepted. We hide our truth in order to create a sense of normalcy and belonging. This can be a very painful existence in that our true nature is one of honesty, connectedness, acceptance and love.

There are five primary coping mechanisms that are used in order to deal with problems or to protect ourselves. Most of us have a natural tendency to use one or more of them:

Fight: Using aggression

Flight: Running away or hiding

Freeze: Becoming paralyzed like a deer in the headlights

Folding: Giving up or giving in; submitting to others

Facing: Asserting oneself; addressing challenges head on

Our innate style of coping is the way we respond to issues of crisis in all areas of life including intimacy. Intimate situations can trigger manipulation and control dramas as explained in Chapter 14. It is helpful to recognize the coping mechanisms you use and set the intention to start facing challenges head on. If you do not, you will perpetuate the problems and experiences of your past.

As a child, I was not encouraged to share my feelings and my truth. As is the case with many children, I was taught it is better to be seen than heard. It was not an environment conducive to cultivating a strong sense of self, nor one that allowed authenticity. Because I was not encouraged to explore who I was, I did not know who I was.

When I met Bob, I thought I was ready for an adult relationship and eventually marriage. However, since I did not intimately know myself, I could not honestly share myself. I had suppressed emotions, unhealed pain and deep-seated shame. My style of coping was to hide (flight) or give in (folding). My anger was turned inward and manifested in the form of hating my body, obsessive compulsive behavior and eating disorders. I had no idea how impossible an intimate relationship would be, until I became conscious of my emotional blocks. Once I became aware of my unhealed hurts, buried feelings and shame, I was ready to release my internal barriers to intimacy.

If you have unhealed trauma or shame, the prospect of intimacy can bring up your greatest fears and expose your deepest wounds. Intimacy will be challenging, if not impossible, if you continue to fall into the habit of the first four coping mechanisms.

Consider your behavior during childhood or past relationships. When you were afraid or when things were not going your way, what did you do? Did you run and hide? Do you get overtly angry? Did you retreat?

The fear of intimacy may be conscious or unconscious. Reasons why we may fear intimacy can include feeling vulnerable, powerless, judged, exposed, overwhelmed, overpowered or smothered. We may also fear potential pain or the loss of autonomy. Many people who have struggled in relationships have a fear of intimacy as well as a fear of abandonment. They create connections with others that are neither too close nor too far. I refer to this dynamic as "reach and withdrawal." I frequently see this in relationships and have participated in the dance myself.

I noticed a pattern in my life in which men would put forth great effort to pursue me while I remained disinterested. Once I became interested, they would disappear. This was very confusing and took some effort to finally understand. Men were drawn to me when I was not quite "available" because I was not quite available to myself. I realized that I had to cultivate a more loving and intimate relationship with myself, and with Spirit, in order for me to end this frustrating pattern.

Many people fear the prospect of intimacy because they fear rejection. It is a potentially devastating prospect to allow ourselves to be vulnerable, deeply seen and then rejected. A heart that is afraid, or hurt, wears a false mask to protect itself from being abandoned, judged or hurt further. It is impossible to have true intimacy if we have an overwhelming need to protect ourselves.

Intimacy does not have to be an all or nothing proposition. It also does not have to be limited to a romantic partner. Intimacy can be experienced with family, friends, co-workers, neighbors and even strangers. We are intimate when we tell the truth about how we feel. To compliment someone's hair, eyes or smile can be an intimate exchange if it is the truth and comes from our heart.

Intimacy involves choice and discernment. It helps to be consciously aware of who we want to share ourselves with and how much we want to share. Our level of intimacy can change daily depending on how we are feeling and who we are with.

Jim and Cindy

The blocks to intimacy are blocks within ourselves. Not being willing or able to speak our truth creates barriers that prevent us from connecting with someone else. The "walls" of unspoken truth can create distance and resentment. I have two clients, "Jim" and "Cindy." During a couples session, Jim mentioned he was feeling disconnected from his wife, Cindy. When speaking of this disconnection, I felt he was withholding something. I encouraged him to speak his truth, he eventually shared his hurt feelings. Jim was disappointed because Cindy changed their evening plans several times in two weeks. He felt Cindy was making her job and her friends a priority over him.

Jim hesitated to share his feelings because he did not want to feel vulnerable. Deep down, he was feeling rejected and abandoned. I encouraged Jim to express his feelings. Once he was able to speak up on his own behalf, he felt more open and connected to himself, and subsequently to Cindy. The wall that prevented Jim from feeling connected to Cindy started to crumble.

When Cindy understood how Jim felt, she was able to address his concerns. She had no idea he felt disappointed and that their plans were so important to him. Cindy promised to be more conscientious in the future. She also offered to arrange something special for that evening.

Until Jim told the truth about how he felt, Cindy could not address his real concerns. Subconsciously, Jim wanted Cindy to just know what he was feeling, reach over the wall of unspoken hurt and remove the obstacles that prevented his experience of connection. However, this was impossible for Cindy to do without Jim taking personal responsibility and speaking up on his own behalf. Jim initially resisted expressing himself because it made him feel like he was being silly, needy and petty (names he was called by his father and older brothers during childhood). The blocks to intimacy remained until Jim could express his personal truth. When he did, his sense of connectedness and intimacy returned almost immediately.

Often we long for an intimate connection with another person because of an internal sense of disconnection and loneliness. Beneath the loneliness is a longing to feel fully present, alive, and to be intimately connected to ourselves and Spirit. Connecting with others is possible only if we are first connected and comfortable with ourselves.

Intimacy requires genuine interest, appreciation and listening with the heart. It also requires a desire to understand and to be understood. It all starts in our relationship with ourselves. We cannot speak our truth if we do not know our truth. Honest communication always begins from within.

We need to be aware of our feelings and honestly communicate our wants, desires, preferences and needs. If someone else is not willing or able to provide what we want or need, often it is because we are not providing it for ourselves. When I meditated on the subject of my failed relationships, I asked Spirit why I could not find someone who understood me. In return, this question came to mind, "Do you understand yourself?" The truth was I did not.

We cannot expect anyone else to understand us if we do not take the time to understand ourselves. An important part of my process included the intention to know, understand, appreciate and accept myself. This paved the way for a relationship with someone who would have the ability and desire to know, understand, appreciate and accept me. The more I accepted and embraced my divine nature, the more it was reflected back to me. The better I treated myself, the better I was treated by others.

When we cultivate an authentically intimate connection with ourselves, we then naturally see the very best in others. Our true nature shines forth and we can openly give and receive love.

Intimacy values honesty, truth and trust. As you start to feel more comfortable and accepting of yourself, you begin to lower your mask. As you lower your mask, you will find others doing the same. Being comfortable in your own skin and being authentically yourself, creates a comfortable space for others to relax and be their true selves. We continue to evolve and unfold through a process of acceptance and joy.

When we are in an intimate relationship with Self and Spirit, we radiate a certain beauty—a beauty that goes beyond the physical. When we love ourselves, we are magnetic and attractive. Supportive and loving relationships occur effortlessly.

I believe intimacy is the source of life. Most of us desire deep connections and friendships with others and loneliness is a state that almost everyone wants to avoid. When we can be alone, yet not lonely, we are cultivating a deeper relationship with ourselves and with Spirit. It is also my belief that God desires us as we desire Him and as we desire one another. If we look deep enough into you or deep enough into me, we find God. Ultimately we are connected at the soul level. It is our true nature and therefore an innate desire, to have a sense of this connection and oneness.

When we reach the destination of self-acceptance, self-love and intimacy, we can participate in a cosmic love affair with the universe. To be open to life is our natural state: to be vulnerable is our ultimate strength. As we cultivate our relationship with intimacy, we will open up to greater levels of connection, awareness, expansion, truth and joy. Once we come to this place of knowing our true nature and adoring ourselves, the world will reflect this back to us and we will most certainly be adored.

Exercise: Cultivating Intimacy

1. Recall an experience when you felt open, intimate and connected with another person.

2. What was this experience like for you? How did you feel? In your journal, describe some of the qualities that were present for you.

3. Keeping those qualities in mind, ask yourself, "Have I ever shared or experienced these qualities with myself." If so, describe when and how.

4. List ways you can share and experience these qualities with yourself.

5. List more ways you can open up to greater levels of intimacy within yourself. Some examples are spending time in nature, meditating, writing your thoughts in a journal, writing a letter to God or doing volunteer work.

6. What would you like to share from your heart with someone else? What would you like to express and to whom? Extending yourself honestly can sometimes bring up a sense of risk or fear. Intimacy can require courage. However, the rewards from heartfelt sharing can be profound.

Exercise: Using Visualization to Cultivate Intimacy

Many people find the following exercise challenging. Although at first it may seem strange and uncomfortable, it will become easier with practice. I recommend revisiting this exercise often and then writing how you feel in your journal afterwards. It is a very powerful and effective way to create a more loving and intimate relationship with yourself.

1. Find a place where you can relax and be comfortable.

2. Imagine you are in a beautiful place, perhaps somewhere in nature or in a sacred environment.

3. Now imagine you are sitting in a chair and across from you is sitting someone who you love, respect and adore. It is your favorite person!

4. Allow this feeling of connection, appreciation, adoration and unconditional love to fill and permeate your being.

5. With these feelings still present in your heart, imagine the person sitting across from you slowly shifting and changing...into you! Allow yourself to continue feeling the same sense of connection, appreciation, respect, adoration and unconditional love towards yourself.

6. Imagine seeing your body and soul radiating remarkable light and beauty. Stay in this place for as long as you are able, breathing love in and out, feeling accepted, appreciated and adored.

Chapter 16
Intentions

A good intention clothes itself with sudden power.
~ Ralph Waldo Emerson

Intention is not something you do, but rather a force that exists
In the universe as an invisible field of energy!
~ Wayne Dyer

Everything that happens in the universe starts with intention—every building ever built, every war ever fought, every great piece of art ever created, even getting a glass of water or preparing a meal requires intention. The act of writing this book and you reading it also began with intention. Intention is a universal law much like gravity. However, unlike gravity, we can choose to consciously work with this powerful universal force or not.

Intention is not necessarily something we do, but rather an important inherent quality of creation. The intention of an acorn is to become an oak tree, just as the intention of a sunflower seed is to become a sunflower. In nature, intention is built in, predetermined and effortless. As human beings we all have the power of choice and the opportunity to work with the creative medium of life. By consciously tapping into the power of intention, we align and co-create with Spirit.

Choosing to work with the power of intention is by far a more effective way of creating the life experiences we desire, rather than the ego-driven tactics of force, manipulation and will. When we attempt to push and fight our way toward a specific result, it is often because of subconscious fear. This fear is a result of not understanding or trusting our true spiritual nature—our power, connection and oneness with God.

Dueling intentions or negative unconscious beliefs can also cause challenges in manifestation. If you want a relationship and say to yourself, "I am going to go out and find that relationship," but you also harbor buried beliefs such as: relationships are hard, all the good ones are taken and I do not deserve love; all the dating services and hard work to find Mr. or Ms. Right will be ineffective. True intention is an energy that invites and allows co-creation. When we understand and utilize the power of intention, we will begin to see dramatic results in our lives. Strong, declared intention sets the universe into motion.

Focused and deliberate intentions require us to clearly and specifically state our desires, envision our ideal situation and cultivate patience and faith. When we do this, a powerful force is invited and called forth. When we are clear about what we want and remove obstacles like fear, competing intentions or resistance, we then become a magnet and a vibrational match for what we have identified. Intentions can be created to achieve any goal, including financial prosperity, opportunities, material things, a deeper and more conscious connection with Spirit, friendships and love.

When I was first introduced to the practice of intention, I was not convinced of its power. I did not believe something so simple could really be that effective. However, I decided to put forth my best effort and be open to the experiment of deliberate intentions. As I considered creating an intention, I chose to start with something simple: "It is my intention to have a good day." Upon reflection at the end of the day, it did seem I had a pretty good day. I thought it was probably a coincidence and did not give it much credence.

Later I started working with health-related issues. I had a history of debilitating chronic fatigue and consulted with many doctors and specialists to help me heal this frustrating and painful health challenge. I started to use the affirmation and intention, "I am wide awake and alert!" and "I am happy and healthy!" I did not immediately feel the results, but after a few days it did indeed seem like I felt a little better. While working with these intentions, I was stating a reality I wanted to call forth and claim, instead of focusing on feeling tired and miserable. After working with my intentions for a while, I had to admit there did seem to be something to this simple practice. I was starting to open my mind to the power of intention.

When we set deliberate intentions, we do not have to know the details of how it will work, when it will manifest or what it is going to look like. We simply need to set the intention and then let the universe do its part. The methods and next steps will naturally reveal themselves. Setting deliberate intentions has the potential to orchestrate infinite possibilities. For example, I set the intention to make money. Without really knowing how I would do it, opportunities started to present themselves in the most extraordinary ways. Although intention will bring you opportunities, you must be willing to take action when it shows up!

Gratitude, patience and faith are important qualities to cultivate while working with intentions. It can be easy to get frustrated when we do not see our intentions immediately realized. There are times when we can speed up the manifestation process by consciously working with our resistance, limiting beliefs and competing intentions. Manifesting what you want is not always as easy as setting an intention, but there are times that it *can* be that simple! Intent can often create amazing coincidence and synchronicity.

Years ago, I set the intention to release my attachment to Bob; heal mentally, physically and emotionally; and come to know myself and God. I had no idea how the process was going to begin, much less come to fruition. However, as soon as I set my intentions, I was supported in remarkable ways. I decided to trust and follow my interests, instincts and feelings. A few years, a lot of education and an amazing husband later, here I am writing about that very process!

It is beneficial to understand and create with conscious intent; otherwise, we end up creating with unconscious intent. Often I see friends and clients manifest what they said they wanted, without realizing or remembering they were the ones who set the intention into motion. I have a wonderful friend, Bill, who had just gotten out of a long, painful relationship and was ready to date again. He set an intention when he told me that he would like to go out with someone without any expectations of a long-term relation-ship—maybe two or three months. Not long after we talked, he met a really cute girl and was having a great time.

A few months later when I saw Bill, he was bummed because the cute girl had just broken up with him. He was sad because he really liked this woman and wanted the relationship to work. I asked Bill how long they had been dating. After some thought, he told me it was three months to the day. I reminded him of his intention and how he was getting exactly what he asked for. I encouraged Bill to refine his request and set a new intention. He said he was a little afraid to ask for what he really wanted, because he did not want to set himself up for disappointment. I said, "Hey! Pretend it's Christmas and ask for what you really want! If you don't ask for what you want, you certainly won't get it!" Bill laughed. He then started to consider what he really, really wanted and what his next intention would be.

People often set a negative intention without realizing it. That happens when we say, "I sure hope this or that doesn't happen," or "I bet this blind date is going to be atrocious." When statements are made in the negative, or when we talk about what we do not want, we are still using the power of intention—but not to our advantage.

When we do not consciously work with the power of intention, we risk attracting things to our life unconsciously as if by default. When our energy is scattered and unfocused, what we manifest in life may seem confusing, chaotic and unfair. The universe reflects back to us what we emit through our conscious and unconscious thoughts and beliefs. If you think you want a relationship, but are afraid you can not have one, you will attract what you do not want. If you think about manifesting a relationship and feel happy, optimistic and excited, then you will easily attract that great relationship. As Carl Jung said, "What we resist persists." If you are more afraid than excited, or more sad than happy, what you will manifest will be more negative than positive.

After my painful break up with Bob, I knew I wanted to be in a supportive, uplifting relationship and even married one day. However, the prospect of a committed relationship caused me a great deal of fear and stress. I chose to explore what was causing the stress and uncovered many irrational thoughts and limiting beliefs. Beyond examining my belief systems, I worked on healing the relationship with myself.

After I cleared out my fearful and limiting thoughts, established my boundaries, knew who I was (and liked who I was), I decided I was ready to meet my husband. I created my powerful, joyful and uplifting intention: "I am attracting the perfect husband for me!" When I thought of manifesting this relationship, I felt happy and optimistic rather than stressed and scared. I then felt ready to create my "Ideal Husband List." I wrote a detailed list of all the qualities and characteristics I wanted my future husband to possess. Creating this list was a powerful way for me to claim multiple intentions to manifest this relationship.

When I created the list of the qualities I wanted my husband to have, I was very specific about his characteristics and the connection we would share. Here are some of the qualities I included on my Ideal Husband List:

We are attracted to one another physically, mentally, emotionally and spiritually.

He is healthy physically, mentally, emotionally and spiritually.

He is family oriented.

He loves and respects his parents.

He is open to having children.

We are best friends!

He loves fine dining and an occasional cocktail.

He does not do drugs.

He has no addictions.

He is happy and comfortable in his own skin.

We are compatible.

Our connection is joyful, easy and fun with no drama!

He loves to travel and has a wonderful sense of adventure.

He is playful.

He is a self-made, very successful business man.

He values money without being frivolous or frugal.

He is refined, chivalrous and well mannered.

He knows to walk on the "street side" of the sidewalk.

He opens doors for me and stands when I leave or come back to the table.

He rubs my feet!

We both love to give generously and receive graciously.

He is kind.

He is patient and non-judgmental.

He is open to my spiritual beliefs but also solid in his own spiritual connection.

He is health conscious but not obsessive. (He likes to work out three to four times a week.)

He is balanced, whole and stable.

My family loves him!

His family loves me!

He is intelligent, ambitious and joyful.

He loves what he does and supports what I do.

He is not jealous or possessive and loves me with an "open hand."

We give each other the space and freedom to explore ourselves and each other.

We share a deep intimacy.

We respect and trust each other.

We allow friendships outside of the relationship.

We make each other laugh!

We communicate well and easily understand each other.

He loves Los Angeles.

He loves my cooking.

He is in touch with his feminine side but he is masculine.

He is sensitive.

He is heterosexual.

He understands politics and world affairs.

He loves animals.

He proposes to me with a beautiful engagement ring.

(Remember it is O.K. to ask for what you want!)

He thinks I am the prettiest girl in the world.

He knows what he wants—and it's me!

After I completed my list, a limiting thought popped into my head, "Men are not like this!" I felt Spirit respond with, "It only takes one!" My trepidation immediately faded away and I laughed—after all, it was true! I easily returned to my optimistic and joyful state. At the bottom of my Ideal Husband List, I invited God in by writing, "For the highest benefit of all concerned." After getting very clear about what I wanted, I then surrendered everything to Spirit.

Surrendering is a crucial part of manifesting intentions. By surrendering, we actually give the situation over to Spirit. We release our attachments and our constrictions. We let go of worry and we relax. We know and accept we are not in control (not that we ever really are). Surrendering creates the space for the God to enter and partner with us on our journey. It is like handing the steering wheel over to Him and then relaxing and enjoying the scenery from the passenger seat. Going about life in this way creates the space for miracles, synchronicity and wonderful unexpected opportunities.

After I set my intentions and invited Spirit in, I felt peaceful, happy and calm. It had been a long road, but I knew I was finally in a loving relationship with myself and with God. I also knew I was going to continue to be happy, healthy, successful and fulfilled, even if my ideal husband did not show up. I was finally enjoying my life and the experience of being me - I was, at last, dancing in my own light.

A Course in Miracles tells us that infinite patience produces immediate results. When we feel relaxed, patient and peaceful, we are not in resistance; we are not pushing or grabbing, nor in desperation or fear. When we are peaceful and optimistic, we are magnetic and in harmony with creation. From this place we can easily draw forth what we desire. When I was finally happy being me and ready to manifest my partner, I knew everything was in order and was simply appreciating life.

About 10 days after completing my Ideal Husband List, I met Steve. Immediately, I sensed I knew him. However, I did not know he would eventually be my husband. I worked for his company as a spokesperson at a trade show where we became friends. After the trade show, Steve went back to his home in Idaho. (By the way, on my Ideal Husband List I wrote that he *loved* Los Angeles. I did not specify that he *lived* in Los Angeles!). We maintained our connection and soon it felt like we were very good friends. He was comfortable in his skin, as I was in mine. We could easily talk about business, philosophy, spirituality, emotional subjects or be completely silly. It seemed we spoke the same language and innately understood each other. Our conversations always flowed. We laughed a lot and our friendship was supportive, sweet and easy. Soon it was apparent to both of us—this was it.

When Steve proposed to me, he offered me a rather substantial diamond engagement ring. In the past, I would have felt overwhelmed by this due to deeply ingrained issues of scarcity and worthlessness. Having worked through my issues of personal value I graciously accepted his proposal and the ring.

In the past, I had wanted things but they always seemed out of reach. I had competing intentions, judgments and subconscious beliefs about being greedy, not being worthy and being indulgent. I had deep-seated judgments about having money or material objects.

One of my big lessons was that it is okay to have desires, money and things. In physical world reality, desire is a part of our nature and material objects are a part of the human experience. However, problems occur when we give too much credence to objects or make the material world our god.

I had a big mountain to climb to overcome my family history. I had distorted views regarding money, scarcity, worthiness and power. I set a deliberate intention to heal these patterns and limiting beliefs. I finally arrived at the healthy, balanced place of knowing that as long as I keep everything in perspective, and make God my priority, I can enjoy everything the world has to offer. The Bible states, "Seek ye first the kingdom of God and all things will be added unto thee." I now easily maintain my balanced state of abundance, connection and joy.

I came across my Ideal Husband List a couple of years after Steve and I got together. I asked if he would like to see it. At first, he seemed to have a little trepidation, but then he said yes. I shared with him all the qualities on my list. When I was done, Steve laughed and said, "That sounds like me!" Yes it did, it was100 percent Steve. My Ideal Husband List is a perfect example of the power of deliberate intention and manifestation.

Now I set intentions daily. I use them to focus on and claim what I want to manifest and experience. I set deliberate intentions as soon as I wake up in the morning—to feel great, to be productive, to be in my joy and to experience synchronicity. Other intentions include connecting with the right people at the right time, to be of service and to uplift and support others. I also set intentions to consciously connect with Spirit, maintain optimal health and weight and create financial prosperity. I use the power of intention to assist me in creating my artwork and writing. I identify and claim what I want to accomplish in meetings, classes and sessions with clients. Intentions can be used for all situations, no matter how large or small. What we think about, feel and intend in the present moment creates an energy and dynamic for what is to come.

Kay's Intentions

I frequently remind friends and clients to set their intentions. I then enjoy observing amazing events unfold. A good friend of mine, Kay, was planning a huge fund-raiser. While planning this event, she felt overwhelmed and depleted. Kay worked hard, doing everything in her power to ensure the success of the event. As devoted as she was to the cause and in spite of how hard she worked, things were not falling into place. Each day there were fires to put out, dilemmas to contend with and major problems to resolve. Kay told me she felt like a salmon swimming upstream. I reminded her she could harness the power of the universe by deliberately setting her intentions. Kay thought about it and then set the intention: "The event will occur with grace and ease and the perfect people will show up at the perfect time to support the cause."

Almost immediately there was a shift in Kay's experience. People began to step up to support her. A company offered free lighting for the event, a great band wanted to perform and free food and drinks were offered by a local restaurant. A pilot offered helicopter rides and vendors donated gift baskets, apparel, vacation weekends, gift certificates and more. People seemed to be showing up out of nowhere to help Kay with this project. She was amazed at how different this experience felt before and after she set her deliberate intention. After Kay declared her intention, the project became easy, productive and fun. Rather than feeling like a salmon swimming upstream, Kay now felt like a surfer riding a huge wave! Through her declaration of intention, Kay partnered with Spirit. Her event went off without a hitch, everyone had a blast and the amount of money raised also exceeded her expectations!

I love reminding people of the power of deliberate intention and supporting them in claiming what they want. It is so exciting to witness the miracles, support and blessings that ensue after deliberate intention has been expressed. The universe is alive, conscious and responds to our intentions. Once we truly comprehend the power of deliberate intention, not only do we have access to a powerful tool, we have greater creative control in manifesting the life of our dreams.

Things to Consider While Creating Deliberate Intentions

You are an important, integral and vital part of the universe!

The universe is designed to support and assist you.

Accept and embrace that you are a powerful creator and you truly deserve all that will make you happy!

Before writing your deliberate intention, go within (pray or meditate) and ask God to help you create your perfect intention.

Enliven your intentions by stating them in the present tense as if they are happening now.

Rather than hoping or wishing, declare your intentions with the energy of certainty and power. For example: "I AM manifesting a loving relationship with the perfect partner for me" or "I AM attracting the perfect relationship for me now."

As you state your intention, allow the positive and energizing feelings of the statement to move through your body. Allow yourself to feel happy, relaxed and optimistic.

After stating your intention, express gratitude. Know that all you want, need and desire is on its way to you in the perfect time and perfect way!

Exercise: Creating Your Ideal Partner List

Earlier in this chapter I shared with you my Ideal Husband List. You may have noticed I included personal qualities and characteristics about him. I also included the type of connection we would share. Now create your own Ideal Partner List!

1. Be specific and ask for what you want. Include all the qualities and characteristics that speak to your heart about the relationship you desire.

2. Keep the descriptions in the present tense, start your sentences out with: "I am," "He (or she) is," and "We are."

3. At the bottom of your list be sure to write: "For the highest benefit of everyone," inviting and surrendering your intention to Spirit.

4. You may want to review your Ideal Partner List once a week. This will keep your intention alive and energized in your heart and mind. You may revise any of the qualities at any time.

5. If you would like, create a vision board. Cut out images from magazines or draw pictures that represent the wonderful relationship that you are ready to claim. This visual, creative, powerful and fun exercise is another way to put out clearly to the universe what it is you desire.

6. The universe responds to imagination in powerful ways. Imagining can be a highly effective way to produce a desired result. If you take the time to go to a place in your heart and mind, you will eventually go there in your life. Imagine, visualize and write in detail about this wonderful relationship and what it will be like. Close your eyes and *really feel* your beloved's arms around you and *feel* the loving connection that you share. Vividly imagine the places you will go and the things that you will do. Visualize the perfect day with your beloved. Write in detail about this wonderful day. Allow yourself to explore and experience all that you desire in this sacred partnership.

There is no greater power than the power of intention. When you have a clear picture of what you want, without any competing intentions, your desires can easily start to take shape and manifest. When you have the full support and endorsement of your emotions, you can attract abundant possibilities. By claiming your intentions and desires, the universe will provide you with opportunities and the next steps on your journey. Deliberate intention has remarkable power and can bring you all the necessary resources in the most mysterious and extraordinary ways!

Chapter 17
Directing Focus

Whether you think you can, or you can't—
you are right.
~ Henry Ford

When you go to a garden do you look at the weeds?
Spend more time with the rose and jasmine.
~ Jelauddin Rumi

A young man was heading to a town he had never been to before. On the outskirts of this town the young man noticed an elderly man and asked, "Excuse me, sir. Are you familiar with this town?" "Yes," replied the old man. The young man then asked, "What are the people like?" The old man responded, "Just like you would think." The young man thought about it and said, "I think they are probably competitive, angry, unhappy people, who don't really want anyone new coming into their town." The wise old man responded, "You are right." And so it was.

Later that day, another traveler was heading into this same town and encountered the same elderly gentleman. This traveler also asked the old man, "Sir, are you familiar with this town?" The old man said, "Yes." The traveler asked, "What are the people like?" The old man once again responded, "Just like you would think." The traveler thought about it and said, "I think they are probably kind, decent people who would be happy to see a new face." The old man responded, "You are right." And so it was.

I had just begun my journey of inner healing when I first heard this parable. It seemed there was some truth to it. I began to realize that I had always gotten (and was continuing to get) what I believed I would all along. Most psychologists agree that our lives move in the direction of our thoughts, beliefs and feelings. If we want to change our life, we have to change our focus. What we imagine wields extraordinary power. Sooner or later those imaginations will likely come to fruition. This will be the case whether your thoughts, beliefs and feelings are positive or negative.

Expecting joy and miracles plants the seeds for joy and miracles. Continually worrying about lack and limitations creates the experience of lack and limitation. Constricted thoughts create constricted experiences; expansive thoughts create expansive experiences. For example, a person who is constantly worried and fearful about finances will never experience great financial abundance, just as a person who knows and believes in their ability to attain financial prosperity will never be broke. We get what we expect; we become what we believe.

Many people believe they have little or no control over the musings of their mind. However, we all have the potential and capacity to shift our thoughts and change the direction of our lives. *A Course in Miracles* tells us, "You accomplish so little because your minds are so undisciplined."

Most of us are not using the power of our minds to our greatest advantage and it is reflected in our lives. Do you have as much money as you want? Do you have the fulfilling relationships that you desire? Are you happy with where you are in your life? If not, there is potential to tap into your own inner resources to alter your experiences and pave the way to manifest what you desire.

We create our self-fulfilling prophecies with our words. Words can limit or propel, prevent or endorse, hurt or heal, constrict or expand. Even in jest our words have power. The universe takes words seriously. Learn to talk about and focus on what you *do* want to invite and endorse, not what you *do not* want to evoke or experience.

When you repeat certain statements like, "Women are angry and competitive," "There are no good men," "I can't afford it," or "Nothing good ever happens to me," you are making a declaration to the universe and creating your reality. If it is not what you want, do not say it! Negative thoughts that are directed towards yourself or others cause unpleasant experiences, disorder and chaos. If what you are thinking about and talking about is not what you want, consider creating a new habit. Do not denigrate yourself and do not focus on the negative. We all have a choice to perceive the glass as half empty or half full. We can focus on the flower in the vase or the dust on the table. When we shift the focus of our thoughts from what we do not want to what we do want, the things we do not want naturally fall away. The things we do want will more easily come forward in our lives.

When I constantly thought about my past, my mistakes and failures, life was indeed unpleasant. As I started making a conscious effort to redirect my focus towards things that were positive and uplifting, my life began to change for the better. Cursing the darkness does not invite the light. Focusing on the light invites in more light! Give yourself the gift of setting the intention to invite the light and affirm the good in your life.

When my relationship with Bob crumbled, I was devastated. I constantly complained about what had happened to me. In my mind, I went over and over what I could have done differently or what it would have been like if we could have made the relationship work. I dissected scenarios in my mind from morning until night. I also discussed the break-up with anyone who would listen.

One of his former girlfriends and I became very good friends. She was very sweet and would listen to me endlessly. We often spent hours talking about Bob and compared our experiences. We were both in a great deal of pain and confusion. We were also struggling with our careers, health and finances. In the meantime, Bob got married, his career soared and I saw him everywhere, on television and in magazines. There was even a billboard of his head erected one block away from my apartment! I thought it seemed so awful and unfair. My life seemed to be getting smaller and more difficult. Meanwhile, his life flourished as he experienced love, fame and worldly success.

As I meditated one day, I asked the question, "Why is my life not moving in the direction I want? Why can I not seem to manifest any of my goals? *And why do I see this man's head everywhere?* The answer came to me. I was simply getting what I was focusing on. I kept talking about how great Bob was doing and how awful I was doing—and so it was.

I began to realize I needed to stop talking, thinking and complaining about all that was wrong with my life. I needed to think, talk and focus on what was right so I could start to move in a more positive direction. Because my focus, thoughts and words were deeply ingrained habits, it took concerted effort to make these changes. I was not immediately successful. When I witnessed myself falling into old patterns, I reminded myself to think or say "No, thank you!" and consciously redirect my focus.

We cannot always control what pops into our minds. We do, however, have control over what we dwell on. When I started to think about Bob or if something unpleasant came to mind, I became aware that I had a choice. I would consciously choose to redirect my focus and think of something different. Often I would choose to think about something I was grateful for, or say a prayer asking for assistance.

Redirecting focus and changing our thoughts from limitation to expansiveness can be challenging. Some doctors believe that neuropathways—the grooves in our brains—are actually created by repetitive thoughts and the habits we entertain. If you have been in a certain "groove" for a long period of time, it may be challenging, if not impossible to simply alter the course all at once. Like water in a river that naturally follows a certain course, it flows in a particular direction and in a particular groove. If you want to change thought patterns, it can be akin to digging a new trench or creating a new river bed. We do this one thought at a time.

You have the power and ability to choose to focus on what is positive in your life and what makes you happy. With each conscious positive thought you are potentially creating a new habit. You start to redirect your river. Although you may not do a full 180-degree turn overnight, it is not unusual to get some immediate positive feedback from the universe that you are going in the right direction. For example, you start to affirm that money is easily coming to and, a short time later, you find a one dollar bill on the ground. You start to repeat an affirmation inviting more love into your life and then hear from a dear friend. You could even be asked out to lunch by an attractive stranger! I believe we get "winks" from the universe. These winks are designed to encourage, prompt and affirm that we are heading in the right direction.

Gratitude

Expressing gratitude is an extremely effective way to redirect focus from the negative to the positive. *It is the most powerful force and the key ingredient in the experience of manifestation.* When you are in discomfort or unhappy, consider the things for which you are grateful. When we are experiencing discomfort or resistance, it is like we are pinched, similar to the pinch in the center of an hourglass. By relaxing and focusing on gratitude, we release resistance and begin to open the pinch. Gratitude brings us back to the present moment, helps us to feel better and supports us in moving in a more positive direction.

If you want to attract more love in your life, consider all of the love you have experienced, all the love in your life currently and all of the love on its way to you now. Relax, breathe, be grateful and receive. Allow yourself to experience the feeling of being wrapped in love, open your heart and feel the gratitude!

One of my students, Samantha, harnessed the power of gratitude to attract her fiancé, Keith. Samantha explains, "Once I cleared out all of my fears, I really invited my beloved in through the practice of gratitude. I wore my grandmother's wedding band on my left hand and frequently thanked Spirit for my wonderful, respectful, loving relationship. I consciously opened my heart and really allowed myself to feel both giving and receiving love. I thanked God daily and even painted a big heart with messages of gratitude in and around it. Shortly thereafter, my former boyfriend, Keith (someone who I still adored), called and told me how much he missed me. We started spending time together and it felt so good. I never would have expected this, but he proposed and we are both so happy. The relationship feels different this time around and I know it is because I now love and respect myself. This whole process has been such an adventure and such a gift. I know I will be practicing gratitude for the rest of my life!" We can't always know where the practice of gratitude will take us, but we can be assured it will be someplace wonderful!

Many spiritual traditions tell us the energy of the universe is that of love and appreciation. When we focus on gratitude, we are lining up with that power. If having a bad day is preventing you from feeling good, bring your focus to your breath and be grateful for the air that is coming in and out of your body. Be grateful that you are not the one doing it—in truth God is breathing you!

Stacey Robin wrote a wonderful book entitled, *Go Gratitude*. In it she wrote, "Imagine being given a master key, yours for all eternity, to open all doors of possibility, rejoice for it is so!" She goes on to say, "Gratitude is the master key and opening passage for opportunity, abundance and celebration."

Maintaining a gratitude journal is another wonderful way to anchor and expand the practice of appreciation. Oprah Winfrey consistently practices gratitude and has kept a gratitude journal since she was a young woman and look what it has done for her!

The Power of Words

The ancient sacred text, the *Bible*, begins with, "In the beginning was the Word." The spoken word carries great power and energy, which creates patterns and experiences. Depending on the words we use, those patterns can be either chaotic and disordered or structured and beautiful.

The remarkable work of Masaru Emoto in his book, *The Hidden Messages in Water*, shows us the literal effect of thoughts and words. His research indicates that water, when exposed to loving words and positive thoughts (such as gratitude or statements like "you're beautiful") create brilliant, symmetrical, complex snowflake-like crystals. In profound contrast, water exposed to negative thoughts or words (such as "you fool" or "you're stupid") forms chaotic, incomplete, distorted and asymmetrical images.

The implications of this research are amazing and prove what many have intuitively felt to be true for years—our thoughts and words literally create our reality. Another profound consideration is our bodies are approximately 80 percent water. Loving, positive thoughts and affirmations directed inward create health, balance, order and beauty on a cellular level. These qualities and attributes are ones that we all could benefit from having more of in our bodies and in our lives.

Positive affirmations are a wonderful way to shift focus, create change and attract opportunities. Affirmations are statements we make to ourselves. Consciously or unconsciously, we use affirmations all the time. When we look in the mirror and think, "I look and feel great," this is a positive affirmation. We are making a negative affirmation when we look in the mirror and think, "I'm an ugly toad and I feel awful!" Both types of declarations create and maintain an emotional state. Whatever we continually affirm will eventually manifest in our lives.

Affirmations work on a conscious level by using our thoughts and minds to make declarations we want to be true. By habitually repeating them, they can end up working their way to the subconscious level where real change occurs. When this happens, we inevitably attract what we affirm.

It is important to become aware of and take responsibility for the musings of our mind, as well as the words that we speak, for they will indeed create our realities. When I started to pay attention to my inner dialogue, I was astonished at how awful I was to myself. Most of my internal conversations were derogatory, mean and extremely negative. I would often say to myself, "I'm a disgusting, fat, ugly pig." I struggled intensely with my weight and appearance. I also attracted people who were not nice to me.

When I started to become more aware of these negative thoughts, I knew the inner dialogue needed to change. When the derogatory banter popped in, I decided to "change the channel" and affirm with "I am a beautiful daughter of God." I imagined myself dancing, looking graceful, thin and elegant. Initially it was strange and difficult, and my relationship with myself did not change overnight; it took time. It took practice and conscious effort to create this new habit, but being nicer to myself coupled with positive inner conversation eventually changed my life. My health improved, I made more money and I attracted much nicer people.

I am now kind to myself on all levels. I know it would have been impossible to manifest a man who adored me if I had not first changed my unkind internal self-talk and learned to adore myself.

It is helpful to set an intention to become more conscious, aware and responsible with your inner and outer communication. New habits take time, so be patient with yourself. Support yourself and write affirmations and messages you would like to claim. Write in your journal about the positive things in your life—what you are grateful for and the accomplishments that make you proud. Write about the things you like about yourself and what you would like more of in your life.

Your thoughts and mind are like the steering wheel of a car; where you direct them, you will go. Consider the direction you want to go and become congruent and consistent in your thoughts, words and actions.

Lee's Story

Lee was a college student. He was concerned he would not be able to attend his final year because of financial constraints. Lee truly wanted to stay in school, yet feared it was not going to be possible. I suggested he redirect his focus and start to express gratitude for currently being in school. I shared with him one of my favorite affirmations: "I am a magnet for magic, miracles and money." (For me, this affirmation plants the seeds for synchronicity and abundance. I have personally manifested incredible results by repeating it.) Lee said he liked the sound of it and would give it a try.

When I saw Lee the following month, he ran over, picked me up and swung me around. He said he had been repeating the affirmation daily. He even put the affirmation on sticky notes all over his apartment and in his car. He told me that about one week into the affirmation experiment, he received a call from the school. An anonymous person gifted him with his last year at the university, so he could complete his education and receive his degree. Lee was amazed by what occurred and the "power" of this affirmation. The power was really within Lee. His willingness to redirect his thoughts by virtue of those words was what paved the way for manifesting this miracle in his life.

Keys for Creating Effective Affirmations

Affirmations are a wonderful and effective tool in promoting change, building confidence and attracting opportunities. To create affirmations that are powerful and effective, you should:

State them in the present tense;

Keep them positive;

Keep them short and simple;

Make sure they are authentic and in your style of speaking; and

State them in a way that supports you in feeling joyful, optimistic using emotionally active words!

Use the present tense. Remember an affirmation is a statement of intention. To effectively communicate with our subconscious mind, they need to be stated in the present tense. The most effective words to begin an affirmation with are I AM. For example, if you want more love in your life, say, "I AM joyfully experiencing love in my life" rather than "I will have more love" or "I want more love in my life."

Keep it positive. Make sure your affirmations are positively charged rather than negatively charged. For example, do not say "I am not lonely." The word lonely appears at the end of this statement and you do not want your subconscious mind to hang onto the negative word or the feeling it conjures up. A more positive statement would be "I am attracting a wonderful, fulfilling relationship." Instead of "I am not sick," say "I am healthy!" Instead of "I am not unhappy," positively affirm with "I am happy!"

Make affirmations short and simple. Keep affirmations short and simple so they can be easily committed to memory. You can repeat your affirmations while waiting in line at the grocery store or sitting in the car while you are stuck in traffic. It is a productive way to use the down time that occurs throughout our day.

Keep it authentic and in your voice. Affirmations should feel uplifting and real. They also need to fit your style of communication. Your affirmations should reflect your preferences, your intentions and your desires. Your mind will more easily accept the statement if you describe what you want in your own way.

Bring about joy and optimism using emotionally active words. Create an affirmation that *feels good* and makes you *happy when you say it!* Do not create one that feels too far fetched or out of the realm of possibilities. If you feel unhappy or frustrated when you repeat your affirmation, chances are it will not be highly effective. For example, if I made the affirmation: "I am a billionaire" it would be unbelievable for me. A more appropriate one (and one that brings me joy) would be: "I am *happily* and *joyfully* manifesting great abundance." If I wanted to claim an actual dollar amount, I could create an affirmation that would double or triple my weekly income. This would be more realistic to my conscious and subconscious mind.

Exercise: Creating Affirmations

1. Create a life affirmation by starting with a catchword or two that feels right and then build your affirmation around it. The following are some examples I have used, enjoyed and had success with:

   I am a magnet for magic, miracles and money!
   Today is a wonderful day!
   I am living in joy and prosperity!
   I am healthy, wealthy and wise!
   I am healed, happy and whole!

2. Now follow the same steps to create a "Love Affirmation." Here are some affirmations I used to manifest my love relationship:

   I am gracefully expanding in love.
   I am joyfully attracting the perfect partner for me.
   I am happily living in profound love and gratitude.
   I am a beautiful magnet for my beloved.
   I am harmoniously aligned with Spirit and attracting great love.

3. After you create your affirmations say them out loud. Your affirmations should be energizing and make you feel good, joyful, optimistic and expansive.

Exercise: Breathing Life into Your Affirmation

1. Write one or more affirmations either in your journal or on an index card.

2. Repeat your affirmations throughout the day. Stating them several times when you wake up creates an intention and the tone for the day. Repeating them before going to sleep can also assist in programming your subconscious mind.

3. Write your affirmations on sticky notes and place them around your house. You may want to place them on your refrigerator, computer screen and bathroom mirrors. In addition you may put sticky notes in your car. This will remind you to repeat and claim your affirmations often.

4. The spoken word has a powerful energy, so say your affirmations out loud. However, if you are in public or in a situation where you cannot, it is fine to repeat them silently to yourself.

5. Using emotionally active words and descriptive words, such as "joyfully, actively, gratefully, easily, harmoniously etc." further activates the affirmation, raises the vibration and makes it *feel good*. This greatly increases the potentail for success.

6. In your journal, record any positive results you get from the universe in response to your affirmation. For exam-

ple, a positive result from your affirmation that you are a "magnet for love" might be a puppy running up to you or an attractive stranger flirts with you in the line at the coffee shop.

7. Express gratitude, this will pave the way for more!

8. Do and say what feels best for you. This is about shifting your focus, making you happy and claiming what you want in your life.

To receive the most value from affirmations, it takes a certain amount of discipline. Your old habits and ways of thinking were established over a long period of time. Developing and cultivating new habits may take some time as well. If you do not see results in a day or two, do not become discouraged. Be patient, have fun and be kind to yourself. If you are willing to spend a little time each day directing your focus, you will see the results and reap remarkable rewards!

Chapter 18
Dreams

*The dream is a little hidden door in the innermost
and most secret recesses of the soul.*
~ Carl Jung

Dreams are today's answers to tomorrow's questions.
~ Edgar Cayce

Dream interpretation has been used throughout history
and dates back to ancient times. The subject of dreaming is
discussed in the *Bible*, the *Talmud*, the *Kabbalah*, The
Tibetan Book of the Dead and other sacred texts. Many people
throughout history have been intrigued, obsessed and
amused by the complex subject of dreaming.

Dreams are powerful tools that can provide us with rich
and wonderful opportunities to explore and understand our
true Self. By choosing to pay attention to dreams, we can
potentially open ourselves to a more expansive way of being
and enhance our creativity and intuition.

Everyone is unique and so are their dreams. We each
have our personal histories, beliefs, experiences, perceptions
and emotions. Every dream we have is connected to our
own personal reality. Dreams speak to us in the language of
symbols; they can be universal and archetypal or they can be
very personal and specific to the dreamer.

One of the most well-known modern dream philosophers, Carl Jung, believed dreams act as a mirror for the ego and reveals what is missing within the consciousness of the dreamer. According to Jung, dreams perform restorative, corrective, compensatory, prophetic and developmental roles in the psyche. Jung wrote that dreams can be our teachers and guides on the path toward wholeness and self actualization. He believed the unconscious is the creative source of all that evolves into the conscious mind and into the total personality.

To become congruent, healthy and whole we need to balance our conscious and unconscious selves. If we do not integrate the unconscious we can end up living blindly and will experience chaos, confusion and disorder. We also end up recreating painful patterns in our lives. Although dreams are not the only way to become more aware of our unconscious material, they are a doorway and present a wonderful opportunity to eavesdrop on the dialogue between the conscious and unconscious mind.

The human mind is like an iceberg—10 percent is above the surface. About 90 percent of an iceberg is hidden beneath water; likewise, about 90 percent of our mental capability is hidden in the unconscious mind. This is why hypnosis and understanding our dreams is so powerful—it allows us to tap into the other 90 percent of our mind. When we integrate the subconscious with the conscious, we are more fully empowered, we get a true sense of who we are and become more complete human beings.

I have been writing down my dreams for a long time but did not always understand how to analyze or process them. However, often when I review them they make a great deal of sense. I recently reviewed a dream I had years ago when I was engaged to Bob.

In this dream, we were on a plane and Bob was the pilot. He was losing control and the plane was rapidly descending. All of my material possessions were flying out of the luggage compartment. When I asked him if he had been drinking, he shouted, "No!" and became angry and defensive. Panicking, I screamed back that he could lose his license and we may even die. I did not know it at the time, but this dream was attempting to communicate important information to me.

My subconscious mind was trying to tell me that the relationship was headed for disaster. I was going to lose my material possessions, there was going to be loss of control and a death to an old way of being. There were many literal and metaphoric layers to this vivid dream. It was a precognitive nightmare that was trying to help me understand a potential outcome if the circumstances of the relationship did not shift. If I had the awareness and ability to process my dreams at that time, perhaps I could have taken a more active and conscious role in the circumstances that would soon disrupt my life. I am amazed by the wisdom of my subconscious mind and what it was attempting to communicate.

Types of Dreams

There are many different types of dreams. I refer to some dreams as junk mail. Other dreams are healing, precognitive, lucid, reoccurring, problem solving, nightmares, archetypal and "out of body" dreams.

Junk mail dreams. These dreams are superficial and non-sensical. They can be caused by extenuating circumstances such as a full bladder, noise in the environment, a fever or indigestion. They can seem disjointed or fragmented and do not tend to contain deep or profound meaning.

Healing dreams. These dreams can alert us to health challenges and even lead to a diagnosis. Our subconscious mind always knows before the conscious mind when there is (or will be) a crisis. If we are willing to work with our dreams, we can take an active part in our healing by using the information, imagery, tools and symbols that present themselves.

Precognitive or psychic dreams. Precognitive means *pre-knowing.* The subconscious mind is not limited to three dimensions and is not bound by time and space. In our dreams, our Higher Self can see the bigger picture and share information with us. Often when we have the experience of *déjà vu* (which literally means "already seen"), it is because we have been there before in our dreams.

Lucid dreams. This is when the dreamer is consciously aware of dreaming. When we are lucid, we have opportunity to direct or control the events and circumstances of our dream. We can get answers, go anywhere and do anything. In lucid dreams, we can alter or participate more fully in the dream experience.

Recurring dreams. When we have the experience of reoccurring dreams or repetitive themes, our subconscious mind is trying to communicate an important message. When these dreams occur, it can be beneficial to examine our thoughts, attitudes and beliefs to determine what is consuming us. This can help us understand the message the subconscious mind is attempting to convey.

Problem-solving dreams. When we are experiencing challenges, answers often present themselves while we are sleeping. The subconscious mind contains vast knowledge and can present information that is inaccessible to the conscious mind.

Nightmares. Nightmares occur when the subconscious mind is urgently trying to get our attention. Often nightmares occur when the subconscious has been unsuccessful in repeatedly trying to relay a message. When we experience recurring nightmares, there is an urgent psychological message in our emotional psyche that needs attention and should not be ignored.

Archetypal dreams. Archetypes are a blueprint for spiritual knowledge and represent basic values inherent in each of us. Archetypes can appear as kings, queens, wizards, mythical creatures, celebrities, cartoon characters, superheroes and more. These characters represent different aspects of ourselves. This type of dream presents an opportunity for us to integrate these aspects in order to achieve wholeness. It can reveal the bigger picture for us as individuals as well as for all of humanity.

"Out of Body" Dreams. These are characterized by a feeling of departure from our physical body and are quite common in the dream state. A dream in which we are able to fly is an example. Out of body experiences enable the observer to see the world from a point of view other than that of being in the physical body.

Some people say they do not dream. According to many scientists, everyone dreams. We either forget them or lack interest in them. When interrupted at the beginning of the REM state (rapid eye movement, the indication of dreaming) and denied the opportunity to dream, people and animals begin hallucinating and exhibit characteristics of insanity.

My friend, Sierra, told me she never dreamed. She did not think there was any reason to dream, much less anything to be learned from them. I was stunned! I shared with her I believe dreams are our teachers and I have received personal messages and truths through them. I also shared some wonderful adventures, remarkable lessons and precognitive messages I have gotten through my dreams. Sierra seemed intrigued. I encouraged her to set an intention to remember a dream that night. The first night, she did not remember anything. The following night, Sierra again set her dream intention and was thrilled the following morning when she actually remembered a dream! As Sierra continued to set her dream intentions she started to experience an interesting and wonderful dream life.

Often dreams can be difficult to recall. We can more easily remember our dreams by setting an intention to pay closer attention to them. As I mentioned in the previous chapter, where we choose to place our attention, is ultimately what will increase in our lives. By showing interest in our dreams, they will come more fully into focus and reveal themselves more clearly.

Writing down our dreams helps us to develop our memory for recalling details. Recording our dreams is the only way to remember them clearly and to learn more about them. I have found that sincere intention is a valuable technique for calling forth, remembering and becoming more conscious of our dreams. Writing the sentence, "Tonight I am having a vivid healing dream that I easily recall in the morning," before going to sleep at night is a powerful invitation to our dreams.

When you wake up in the morning, remain still. When you move, dreams can easily slip away. Try to recall any images or experiences. If you do not remember anything, simply maintain your intention, do it again the next evening and continue with the process. In time, you will remember your dreams.

When you are able to recall your dreams, write them down, even if it is just a few words. You may discover as you write, you remember more details. You may want to reflect on the dream immediately, or you may want to read and interpret it later. Often I have written dreams down and thought they made no sense. However, when I reviewed them at a later time, the messages and wisdom were abundantly clear.

If you have interest in interpreting dreams, avoid using a dream dictionary, as dreams are far too subjective and personal. You are your own expert. You are the creator of your own symbolic language. It is important for you to decipher its meaning. This will assist you in understanding the messages of your own personal parables.

In my experience, one of the most powerful dream interpretation techniques was developed by Fritz Perls, a noted German psychiatrist and psychotherapist. Perls proposed that because we are the creator and dreamer of our dreams, everything in our dreams—characters and even objects—represents an aspect of ourselves.

I suggested to Julie, my client who had the dream about the cherry pies (Chapter 8), that we explore her dream using Perls' technique. I asked Julie to imagine herself as each of the different symbols in her dream—the couch, the rotten cherry pie and the fresh cherry pie. She thought I was crazy, but decided to go along with the process. I asked Julie to describe herself in first person and in present tense as each symbol. For example, I asked her to "be" the couch and describe herself. Julie laughed and agreed to give it a try. She said, "I am a couch. I am colorful, a little bit worn down, unique and fairly comfortable. I am pretty stable and I like it when I can support people." Julie laughed again and admitted this was a very accurate description of herself.

I then asked Julie to "be" the rotten cherry pie. She said, "I am a cherry pie. I want to be fresh and beautiful. I want to make people happy and nourish them, but I can't because I am old, rotten and disgusting." Tears welled up in her eyes. I encouraged her to let them flow. When her tears subsided, I asked her to finally "be" the fresh cherry pie. She began, "I am a cherry pie and I am hiding behind the couch. I am waiting to be discovered. I have been around forever. I am clean, fresh, wonderful and beautiful. I am ageless and eternal, pristine and incredible. I am perfection."

Once again, Julie experienced a great deal of emotion as she felt her way through the process.

Although Julie was initially skeptical, she was willing to admit that her revelations were profound. She learned valuable things about herself. This way of processing dreams may sound simple - and it is. It is also extraordinarily powerful and healing. I have witnessed many clients experience intense emotions, incredible epiphanies and deep healing as they reflect, explore and "become" the different symbols presented in their dreams.

When you set a dream intention or make a request for information in regard to a specific situation, this is referred to as *incubating* a dream. After I created my Ideal Husband List, I felt I was ready to meet my husband. I decided to incubate a dream for clarity. Within a few days, I had several vivid dreams. In one of my dreams I descended into a tunnel that was long, dark and dirty. I was alone and scared. After traveling for quite some time, I noticed light at the end of the tunnel. As I emerged from the darkness, I felt much better. I then noticed a man with dark hair waiting for me. I recognized him immediately and jumped into his arms. I remember saying, "I didn't think I was going to see you this time." I felt love, connection, familiarity and joy.

In my dream, I was all of the aspects and characters—me, the tunnel, the light at the end of the tunnel and the other person I encountered. In describing myself as the tunnel I said, "I am a hard container. I am constricted, dark and depressed. I feel uncomfortable, alone and confused." I then explored being the light and said, "I am moving out of my constricted way of being. I am stepping into my light. I am remembering the truth of who I am. I am one with Spirit, I am the light." Next, I described myself as the man I encountered and said, "I am strong, balanced and remembering my wholeness. I am connected and aligned. I am in my joy."

As I interpreted my dream, I understood that I had done a great deal of healing. I was becoming more balanced, whole and integrated. In retrospect, this dream was also precognitive. I met my future husband later that week and, just as I had written on my Ideal Husband List, I did indeed "recognize" him.

It takes courage to explore our dreams and the depths of our psyche, for they will reveal hidden truths about ourselves. Dreams always tell the truth about what we think and how we feel. If we try to suppress or deny aspects of ourselves, they will be revealed through our dreams. Choosing to be conscious of our dreams is really about waking up and becoming more conscious and aware. Our subconscious mind knows things we do not, and by paying attention, we can put ourselves on the fast track to personal growth.

Exercise: Having and Recalling Dreams

1. *Invite dreams.* Do not hunt, attempt to control, or capture your dreams. Dreams respond much better to invitation and intention rather than force.

2. *Dream intention.* Write down an intention to vividly recall your dreams.

3. *Dream incubation.* Write down your request for clarification about a specific subject right before you go to sleep.

4. *Recall the dreams you receive.* When you wake up from a dream, lie still for a moment and review it. Allow the dream to reveal itself and the pieces to come together.

5. *Write down your dreams.* After you have reflected on your dream and remember as much as you can, write down all you can recall. More details of the dream may surface as you are writing.

6. *Keep a tape recorder by your bed.* It is much easier for some people to turn on a tape recorder and talk about a dream, than to turn on the light and write it down. Experiment and see what works best for you.

7. *Keep a dream journal.* This practice is a good way to encourage dreaming and stimulate recall. Reviewing the journal at a later date can help you to further understand your dreams and any patterns or ongoing themes in your life.

Exercise: Exploring Your Dreams

1. *Explore being every character in your dream.* Just as Julie "became" every symbol in her dream, try to be every person and object in your dream. Speak in the first person and the present tense. Let your imagination run wild without editing or becoming too analytical.

2. *Consider how the dream makes you feel.* Often how we feel in a dream is its most revealing aspect. How do you feel about the different people, animals or objects? Feeling our way through dreams is often much more effective than thinking our way through them.

3. *Free association.* Make a list of free associations about the different characters and objects that appear in your dreams. You can obtain greater clarity regarding the symbolism and relationships within your dreams by using this technique.

4. *Dialogue with your dreams.* Sit in a chair and imagine the objects or characters of your dream in another chair. Talk with them. Ask them questions. Then switch chairs and allow them to respond to you and through you. For exam-

ple; if you were riding a bike in a dream and hit a tree, talk to the bike or tree. Let them respond to you and reveal their personal messages and meanings. Allow the process to be spontaneous. You may be amazed at what you learn.

5. *Talk about your dreams.* Share your dreams with a friend. Sometimes when we talk about our dreams, we experience epiphanies, clarity and a deeper understanding. Also, our friends may clearly see a message we may have missed.

Dreams are stories from your Higher Self you can ignore or invite; avoid or embrace. You can sleep through your dreams or awaken with them. If you choose to pay attention and integrate the personal messages received through your dreams, it can lead to profound healing. When you are whole within, you are much more apt to manifest a healthy, supportive and loving relationship. By becoming more integrated and aligned through the process of understanding your dreams, the more prepared you are for manifesting the greatest love of your life.

Chapter 19
Meditation

Be still and know that I am God.
~ 46th Psalm, verse 10

Meditation is the straight flight of the mind to the
Kingdom of heaven present in the heart of everybody.
~ Maharishi Mahesh Yogi

The mind is extraordinarily powerful. As human beings, we tend to have many random thoughts, which can create chaos in our minds. As discussed in previous chapters, inner reality is reflected back to us in our outer reality. The chaos of our minds will inevitably manifest as chaos in our lives.

Meditation creates space by clearing the chatter of our thoughts. When you still your mind, you easily come into alignment with your Higher Self. From this place of inner peace and connection, you are able to access deep inner wisdom, clarity and intuition. Meditation is ultimately about cultivating an intimate connection with yourself and Spirit.

My personal meditation practice started out of necessity. I was experiencing panic attacks, anxiety and depression and my body rejected antidepressants and other medications that are normally prescribed to treat these conditions. When I heard about the benefits of meditation, I decided to give it a try and started a simple practice. For 10 to 20 minutes in the morning, I focused on my breath. At first it seemed as though nothing was happening, but eventually I began to notice a pattern. On the days I meditated I felt more peaceful and balanced. I also seemed to experience more meaningful coincidences. On the days I did not meditate, my anxiety and depression seemed to return. There was an undeniable link between my meditation practice and how I experienced my life. During one session, I came to realize that if I meditated consistently for five minutes a day, it would significantly change my life for the better.

Research on meditation and the brain have produced evidence that we change the workings of the mind and are able to achieve greater levels of awareness when we meditate (Antoine Lutz, Lawrence Greishar, Nancy B. Rawlings, Matthew Ricard and Richard J. Davidson, "Long-term mediations self-induce high-amplitude gamma synchrony during mental practice," *Proceedings of the National Academy of Sciences*, 101, no. 46 (2004): 16369-73.). Researchers have found longtime practitioners of meditation show levels of brain activity that have never been documented before. In addition, the area of the brain associated with happiness—the left prefrontal cortex—is much more active in those who meditate compared to those who do not. These studies indicate meditation can improve our levels of happiness, mental activity, focus, memory, cognitive learning and consciousness.

I often use meditation to help me clarify certain situations. A few years ago, I was apprehensive about accepting a spokesperson job, in which I was asked to work lengthy hours at a trade show. Trade show work is notoriously exhausting and, with my history of chronic fatigue, the prospect of this work seemed particularly daunting. I meditated about the situation and realized if I took the job, I could invite and receive divine nurturance at any time and be replenished. I decided to accept the job. I meditated at the beginning of the show and set my intention to receive divine nurturance. During the day, I would close my eyes for just a moment, relax and visualize light pouring into me. I also took short meditation breaks throughout the day. It worked amazingly well. At the end of the show, my colleagues could not understand why they were completely exhausted while I appeared to be refreshed and energized. It was because of my intention, meditations and visualizations. They were like healing balms to my body, mind and soul.

Here are some benefits that practitioners of meditation have experienced:

Increased energy

Increased awareness

Being more present

Improved focus

Experiencing centeredness, wholeness and a sense of peace

Balance and harmony

Increased sense of connection, fulfillment and well-being

Clarity about life's purpose

Increased intuition

Synchronicity

More easily manifesting desires

Greater sense of peace and joy

Reduced anxiety, loneliness, depression or despair

More restful sleep

Healing physically, mentally, emotionally and spiritually

Aligning with one's Higher Self

Opening one's heart

Experiencing and attracting love

The reasons to meditate are varied and numerous. Just as exercise is good for the body, meditation is good for the heart, mind and soul. We are all sparks of God and meditation is the process of visiting, expanding and aligning with the "God spark" that resides within.

I believe there is truth in the old adage, "Prayer is talking to God; meditation is listening to God." Imagine picking up the phone and calling a loving, patient and wise friend. Now imagine spewing all of your problems and desires and, without waiting for their response, you hang up. Don't you want to hear what they have to say? We greatly benefit when we take time to meditate and "listen" to God's input. During meditation, we have the opportunity to sit one-on-one with Spirit, and receive messages exclusively for us.

Almost everyone I know resists meditation, including myself. Often it seems the more we need it, the more we resist it. When I encounter friends or clients in great discomfort, I will ask them if they have considered meditating. Frequently their response is something like, "I can't sit still; I'll go crazy." No, they are going crazy because they are not sitting still! I have been guilty of this same type of behavior. In the past, I thought, "If I go fast enough, I can get away from myself and out run the pain." It did not work. No matter how fast I went, I could not out run myself—the pain and spiritual emptiness persisted.

The more we try to run away from ourselves the more likely we are to have accidents or illness. A powerful way to heal frustration, anxiety and emptiness is by reconnecting with our center and our spiritual essence. Relief is within and can be accessed by meditation.

Often when I suggest meditation to someone who has not tried it or is unfamiliar with the process, the most common excuse I hear for not doing it is, "My mind is too active. I can't *not* think." Meditation is the experience of directed focus, not spacing out as some might believe. A wonderful way to start a meditation is to direct the energy of the mind rather than quiet it. This can be done in the form of counting your breaths or silently repeating mantras or chants. Usually after a minute or two of directed focus, the mind easily and naturally starts to slow down and relax.

For me, one of the most wonderful benefits of meditation is synchronicity. Carl Jung coined the term *synchronicity* which means "meaningful coincidence." I am always amused by how these coincidences seem to be directly related to my meditation practice. These coincidences make me laugh—it is as if God is winking at me. I experience a sense that all is well. For example, after a morning of meditation, I was driving along and thinking about writing this book. I noticed a billboard that read, "Just Do It!" I laughed and thought, "Hmm, I wonder how I would go about writing a book?" Immediately a car pulled in front of me with a bumper sticker that read, "With God All Things Are Possible!" If I had not meditated that day, I doubt I would have noticed the billboard and I probably would have gotten angry at the guy that pulled in front of me.

When I take the time to meditate, I experience grace and synchronicity throughout the day. For example, I might envision a friend's face during meditation. Later that day, I will receive a call from them. Often, I will think about a song and will hear it on the radio moments later.

A wonderful friend of mine recently decided to start a meditation practice. Her practice involved repeating the mantra, "I am living in grace." A few days later she received an article of clothing from another friend with the words "I Love Grace" on it. Later that evening she went on a dinner date. The gentleman, who was unaware of her new meditation practice, brought her to a restaurant named Grace. She had meditated on grace and received immediate feedback from the Universe! To her, it was confirmation the mantra she repeated during her meditation was heard. She, too, felt she received her wink.

There are many types of meditation; the originations of which stem from varied philosophies and religions. Meditation is a highly personal experience and there are as many variations of meditation as there are people. Meditation is an expression of our deepest essence. As with anything, meditation takes practice. You would not expect to go to the gym once and instantly expect to have the perfect body, would you? If you think you cannot meditate, it is probably because you have not found a way that works for you. However, if you can daydream, imagine or have a conversation with yourself, you can meditate. Everybody has the capacity to reflect inwardly.

To find a style that works for you, it helps to understand how you think by determining what senses you rely on the most. Some different ways people process information are visually, auditorily and kinesthetically. When considering what you did yesterday, do you "see" what you did? If so, you are visually oriented. If you hear commentaries in your thoughts, you are auditorily oriented. If you feel the experience or have to move your body to activate the memory, you are kinesthetically oriented. You may primarily rely on one of your senses or use a combination of them. The following examples are meditations that apply to the different senses. See if any of the following types of meditation appeal to you. Remember, there is no right or wrong way to meditate and by simply taking the time to try it (even if you think you are not doing it well) you will reap wonderful benefits and rewards.

Types of Meditation

Breathing meditation. This simple and universal meditation involves focusing on the experience of breathing. Close your eyes and simply observe your breath. Pay attention to the air coming in and out of your nostrils, the temperature of the air and how it feels. Notice your lungs filling with air. Do not change your breathing, simply become aware of it. As you pay attention, your breathing may slow down and become deeper. When we focus on our breathing, we tend to relax our bodies and minds. A greater flow of oxygen is distributed throughout the body. The breathing meditation is an effective way of calming and soothing ourselves. It also assists us in attaining greater focus, balance, peace and awareness.

Visual meditation. When you focus on an imagined person or scenario and allow yourself to relax and become centered, this can lead to a meditative state. You can envision a spiritual teacher, a young child, an animal, or pet that evokes a sense of joy, purity or gratitude. The image of light is also a powerful visual meditation tool. You can imagine a ball of healing light in the center of your being, or you can surround yourself with a glowing light. You may choose to create an inner sanctuary, or imagine a beautiful place in nature. Perhaps you feel a sense of connection sitting next to a stream, in a forest, on a mountain or by the ocean. If you are a visually oriented person, this type of meditative practice is very powerful and an effective way of focusing and relaxing the thinking mind. It can also assist you in connecting with your Higher Self and expanding your consciousness.

Object focus meditation. Focusing on a sacred object with your eyelids slightly lowered to relax into a meditative state is the premise of object focus meditation. You may choose an object such as a candle flame, picture, crystal or something from nature. You will want to select a symbol you find beautiful, calming and creates a sense of appreciation. If you find yourself stressed out, you can reconnect to the sacred and peaceful place within by simply focusing your awareness on a sacred object and allowing yourself to breathe deeply and relax.

Chanting or mantra meditation. This is an ancient practice that focuses the energy of the mind and aids in accessing the spiritual world. When you repetitively chant a word out loud, it vibrates throughout your energy field and raises your vibration to a higher frequency. Chanting balances the subtle energy system and has the potential to bring you to a deep state of meditation. The most widely used Sanskrit mantra is *Om* (the universal sound), or Hu (pronounced "hue") meaning Divine Love. Some people choose to chant the word God. One of my favorite chants is *Om Namah Shivaya* (pronounced Om Namyah Shiv–a-yah) which is Sanskrit for "I bow to the divine within." Chanting is a powerful meditation technique that can help you anchor your awareness and quiet your mind.

Affirmation meditation. This meditation involves the repetition of a phrase or affirmation either silently or out loud. You may create your own mantra, or you may choose to focus on a message from the Bible or another sacred text. By synchronizing your breath with your mantra, you can energize this meditation. For example, using the mantra, "I am aligned and whole." Inhale while thinking or saying the words, "I am." Exhale while thinking or saying the words, "aligned and whole." During this meditation, you may receive visual images, feelings or impressions.

Music mediation. As the name suggests, music is the focal point of this meditation. Choose gentle, soothing music that promotes and encourages peace and harmony.

This can be a great meditation practice for those who are auditory in nature and enjoy music.

Guided meditation. There are many CDs available that use sound, music and imagery to assist listeners on guided inner journeys. The subject matter is varied and there are many options available. This is a great tool for people who want support focusing their attention or find other practices challenging.

Gratitude meditation. Gratitude is a powerful way of opening one's heart and assists in accessing the deep place of peace and reverence within. You can tap into heartfelt gratitude by simply focusing, one by one, on the things you are truly thankful for in your life.

Walking meditation. This type of meditation requires focusing on the movement of the body. Smaller steps are usually taken and the feet are placed consciously, rhythmically and slowly on the ground with every step. Extreme focus is paid to the feeling of your feet touching the ground, the physical movement of your body and your breathing.

Mandala meditation. My favorite type of meditation is focusing on, or creating a mandala. *Mandala* is a Sanskrit word meaning "sacred circle." They can include various geometric designs (usually circular) and symbolize the universe and wholeness. Mandalas have been used for centuries in many cultures and traditions as a medita-

The Sri Yantra, or Yantra of Creation, is a powerful mandala from the Hindu tradition. It represents the timeless creative principle and has been used for centuries as an object of meditation and for the purpose of healing body, mind and spirit.

tion tool. They have also been used for the purpose of healing, self revelation, awareness and connection with Spirit. Carl Jung worked extensively with mandalas, both personally and in his practice. He considered them to be the most powerful tool to understand, express and heal oneself. He referred to them as "the archetype of wholeness." By meditating on a mandala or through the creation of one, we have the potential to relax, heal and become more whole.

Chakra Meditation. The word *chakra* is Sanskrit for "wheel." According to yoga philosophy, a chakra is one of several centers of spiritual energy within the human body. They are arranged vertically from the base of the spine to the crown of the head. If you could see chakras (as many psychics do) you would observe vortexes of energy and colors. Focusing on the chakras during meditation helps us to connect within and is an effective way to achieve inner balance. Similar to the body's physical energy centers—heart, lungs and brain—our subtle body has seven main energy centers (chakras). Each has its own color, qualities and sound. You can use any or all of your senses to balance and open the chakras.

The *root chakra* is located at the base of the spine and is the chakra of manifestation and survival. It is connected to tribal programming, which is the information our families have handed down to us as our primal needs. This chakra regulates our physical existence, connection to the world and basic needs. If you are struggling financially, not living in a home you love or driving a car you enjoy, you probably have a constriction in the root chakra. Such a constriction can also bring about physical challenges related to weight, adrenals, legs and feet. The color of this chakra is red and the sound is "lam." (All of the chakra sounds rhyme with "aum.")

The *sacral chakra* is located just below the belly button. It is the seat of intimacy, the energy center of change and the foundation for relationships. The sacral chakra is closely associated with feelings, sensuality, procreation and creativity. The qualities of this chakra are gentler than the primal qualities of the root chakra. It also is the center in which we experience "gut feelings," empathy and self-judgment. Physical problems that may stem from the constriction of this chakra are kidney or bladder problems, a stiff lower back, sexual problems, fertility issues, PMS, colitis and appendicitis. Other challenges may come in the form of creative blocks and co-dependency. The color of this chakra is orange and the sound is "vam."

The *solar plexus chakra* is located in the stomach region. It is commonly known as the power center and is the vortex of transformation and personal boundaries. It functions as the storehouse for creative expression and the place where judgment of others, opinions and beliefs from our family of origin reside. The solar plexus chakra also relates to confidence, self esteem, insecurity, control dramas and people pleasing. Physical symptoms from an imbalance in this chakra may include digestive disorders, ulcers, diabetes and hypoglycemia. The color of this chakra is yellow and the sound is "ram."

The *heart chakra* is located in the chest and is often referred to as the chakra of love and compassion. It is the storehouse of our innermost dreams and desires. It is also the energy center of heart connections, honor, integrity and emotional healing. The heart chakra influences our ability to give and receive graciously. It is the door to intimacy and influences our ability to connect deeply and authentically with others. Constrictions can take the form of heart problems, sleep disorders, high blood pressure and lung-related problems. The color of this chakra is green and the sound is "yam."

The *throat chakra* is often referred to as the chakra of creativity. It is the energy center responsible for communication, self-expression and self-protection. It is the chakra that supports us in speaking our truth and the primary chakra associated with responsibility. Disorders that affect the throat, mouth, jaw, tonsils, thyroid and thymus may be related to constriction in this chakra. Imbalances may also cause stiff necks, frequent colds and hearing problems. The color of this chakra is blue and the sound is "ham."

The *third-eye chakra* is located in the center of the forehead. It is the energy center of intuition, imagination and clear vision (clairvoyance). It is linked to the pituitary gland, which regulates many of our hormonal and endocrine functions. Problems related to constrictions in this chakra may manifest in issues regarding vision, headaches, hormonal imbalances, growth and development challenges. The color of this chakra is indigo or purple and the sound is "aum."

The *crown chakra* is located at the crown of the head and is associated with higher consciousness and transcendence. The crown chakra is the energy center through which we connect with the universe and God. Problems related to this chakra may manifest in the form of cancers, problems with bones, the nervous system and dizziness. Imbalances in the crown chakra may also be associated with learning disorders, neurosis, depression and a lack of self-understanding or direction. The color of this chakra is clear or white. Some scholars believe the sound of the chakra is "ah," while others believe there is no associated sound.

To be able to manifest and live a balanced, joy-filled life, it is important to have all the chakras open and functioning. My goal was (and continues to be) to evolve, so when I first learned about chakras and meditation I chose to focus on opening my higher chakras. Because I worked exclusively with my upper chakras, I ended up feeling imbalanced and disoriented. I was involved in several automobile accidents. I also had a hard time making money and finding a home. Working with the lower chakras helped me to get back into my body and deal with earthly issues such as generating income and everyday life.

For the higher chakras to be open, balanced and fully functioning, we need to have the lower chakras open, balanced and fully functioning. I recommend tuning in and opening each of them, working your way from the root chakra up to the crown chakra. Spend as much time as you need; visualize each of the colors and sounds of the chakras before progressing to the next. Work with your chakras until you feel grounded,centered, open and peaceful.

There are many techniques you can use to achieve a feeling of inner balance. One is to imagine scanning yourself with discs of light spinning in front of, through and behind you. Use your intuition to determine which of the chakras may need extra attention. To strengthen and balance each chakra, imagine each one expanding and aligning with the others. This is a wonderful way of tuning into yourself, conducting an intuitive health check and enhancing your spiritual fitness.

Meditation Suggestions

Meditating first thing in the morning is a wonderful way to start the day. This is the time when the mind is most open to receiving new impressions. It is also when we have the opportunity to intentionally create our day, enhanced by a more balanced, connected, whole and joyful state. *A Course in Miracles* tells us that five minutes spent with God in the morning guarantees He will be in charge of our thoughts throughout the day. Most of us would not consider going out into the world without first cleansing our physical bodies. Imagine how much we would benefit from cleansing our energy field and mind.

The end of the day is also an excellent time to meditate. After all your activities and obligations have been fulfilled, take some time to go within and find your center—a peaceful inner sanctuary. Focusing on gratitude and peace can assist you in sleeping soundly and deeply.

A few minutes of meditation any time during the day can be of great benefit. When you choose to quiet your mind and bring your energy back into your self, it is a powerful step toward inner peace, clarity and balance. The more you practice inner stillness, the more aligned and connected you will feel with the world. Forces you have not been consciously aware of will begin to move toward you and support you in unforeseen and miraculous ways!

Posture. The posture you assume during meditation is important. You should be comfortable. You may choose to sit cross-legged on the floor, on a pillow, or on a couch or chair. Slumping or slouching should be avoided; your spine should be erect and extended. Lying down is also an option, but not always the best choice as you may become too comfortable and fall asleep.

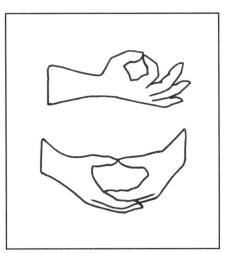

Two examples of mudras are the Chin Mudra (top) and the Dhyana Mudra (bottom).

If you like, there are universally used hand positions, called *mudras,* that can be used to signify that you are going into a meditative state. Two commom mudras are the Chin Mudra and the Dhyana Mudra. For the Chin Mudra, use your thumb and first finger to form a circle, the other three fingers are relaxed and extended. For the Dhyana Mudra, allow your hands to form a cup or bowl, with the thumbs touching at the tip, or slightly overlapped. With both of these mudras allow your hands to rest comfortably on your thighs. When your hands are in these positions the energy circuits are connected. The flow of energy, or *chi*, moves continuously through your body.

Ask questions. Often I begin my meditation ritual by praying. I say everything I want to say, express gratitude and then allow my mind to relax and become still. Once I feel my mind is silenced through focusing on my breath or visualizing light, I will ask a question. Practicing this type of meditation is how I have received some of my greatest revelations. This is how I open my heart to "hearing" God. Whenever I am confused about something, I quiet my mind, pose a question and always receive an answer. This reassures me I have the ability to communicate directly with Spirit. I have never been ignored and I am certain the messages and wisdom come from something much greater than my own conscious, thinking mind. If you are confused and have a question, use whatever method calls to you. Once your mind becomes still, ask your question and be open to receiving the wisdom, support and guidance that comes forth.

Write things down. It can be helpful to have a pen and paper with you during your meditation practice. If you find your mind continues to think about all the things you need to do—such as errands, appointments and chores—take a moment to write these things down. Your mind can more easily relax knowing it has been heard. After you have done this, gently return your focus to your meditation. You also may want to have your journal with you so you may write down any epiphanies that come to you during the meditation process.

Practice. With practice, meditation can assist you in becoming more happy, calm and loving. It also can assist you in becoming more clear about who you are, your value and contribution to the world. Once you have tapped into and connect with your inner wisdom and wholeness, you can easily attract amazing experiences in your life. You also become a conduit for powerful healing energy.

Once you find a type of meditation you enjoy, do not think you must limit yourself to just that one style. Allow your meditations to vary and evolve. Your inner life, connection to your Higher Self and your relationship to Spirit can deepen, expand and come alive during your meditation practice. Experimenting and exploring is highly recommended and can be interesting, beneficial and educational.

Often the human experience can be lonely and life can feel like a monologue. When we start a meditation practice, we open our hearts and life starts to feel more like a dialogue. We can see, feel and hear Spirit speaking to us in our hearts, through people, situations, synchronicities, miracles, opportunities and events. Meditation is one of the most powerful tools we have to access our body's innate healing capabilities and to tap into universal intelligence. It is a pathway to inspiration and freedom. Through meditation we invite and evoke internal and eternal wisdom and cultivate a deep personal relationship with God. A sustained meditation practice not only supports us in evolving and healing, but assists us in living a more divinely led, joy-filled and love-filled life.

Chapter 20.
Happily Ever After... The Sequel

Love does not consist in gazing at each other,
but in looking outward together in the same direction.
~ Antoine de Sainte Exupery

A sacred partnership draws its passion from its inclusiveness.
Passion for another has to fade,
but passion for life itself is eternal.
~ Deepak Chopra

Yes, most of us yearn for true love. We long to merge with another and dance in concert, but should "happily ever after" be our goal? Is it even a possibility? Or is it a myth we should just let go of and forget about? Would we be better off changing the end of our stories to, "...and they lived a fairly decent life?"

I do believe in happily ever after, but, in my case, perfect love did not come in the form of a white knight rushing to my rescue. Nor was it because I found *The One*. I believe I have been able to find happiness and manifest true love because I: 1) took personal responsibility for my healing; 2) learned to love myself unconditionally; and 3) cultivated a deep relationship to the source of Divine love within.

We are all entitled to perfect love, but human beings are flawed. Believing we will find love outside of ourselves inevitably sets us up for frustration and disappointment. That being said, the love that resides within us is perfect; it is the wellspring of Spirit that exists in the very center of our being. Once we understand this and tap into it, we can attract someone else who has tapped into it as well. In these types of relationships, we can experience moments of Divine love being channeled through human form.

The path to love and achieving "happily ever after" is ultimately a personal process. When you align with your Authentic Self and find the place of genuine comfort within, true love can naturally and easily show up in your life. Your beloved can take the form of a friend, a lover or partner that you can continue to venture forth with on the journey of personal revelation, joy and healing. A relationship created from two individuals who have come to the place of self-understanding, self-acceptance and self-appreciation, have the potential to experience adventures and fulfillment like no other type of partnership.

People often mention what a great couple Steve and I are and I would absolutely agree. Our connection is easy, respectful, patient and kind. We laugh, play and hold the space for each other to explore who we are as individuals and as a couple. We are clear in our boundaries, respect one another and lift each other up.

As I reflect on the work I did to manifest this remarkable relationship, I acknowledge the diligence, faith and courage it took. Patience, fortitude, compassion and strong intention were my constant companions. I equate my healing journey to that of demolishing a house. It had to be torn down to the ground and then I built a new foundation that was strong, solid and able to withstand any storm.

To attract this relationship, I had to go into the pain of my past and rescue myself. I had to forgive everyone that hurt me (including myself), get in touch with my feelings and culti-vate healthy boundaries. I also found ways to give myself all I wanted and needed as a child but did not receive. I had to bring love and compassion to the aspects of myself I deemed unlovable. This inner work, combined with cultivating an inti-mate connection with Spirit, is what created my rock-solid foundation for manifesting love. Although at times I was scared and the journey seemed daunting, the reward for say-ing "yes" to my healing process far exceeded anything I could have imagined, dreamed of or hoped for.

If you have had the patience and courage to complete the exercises outlined in this book, you probably learned a great deal about yourself. You also may have learned the most important lesson in how to manifest true love: It con-sists of finding the safe, sacred place within and learning to authentically love yourself. You will then be like a magnet that attracts sacred partnership.

The qualities and tools you use to heal and come into loving relationship with yourself, are the very same qualities and tools you use to manifest, nurture and maintain loving relationships. When you succeed in deepening your connec-tion with your Self and Spirit, you have the very real oppor-tunity to experience heaven on earth.

In Summary

Cultivate your relationship with Spirit. This relationship is the foundation for all of the other relationships in our lives. Meditation assists in further cultivating this relationship and helps us maintain a sense of peace and equilibrium. Find the sacred space within—your safe haven in any storm. Find the place within where you feel connected to your heart, Higher Self and to Spirit. Go there often. Enjoy feeling and knowing you are safe, loved and free. Refilling our "inner well" happens more easily when we take the time to be with ourselves and God in this sacred way.

Take responsibility for your own healing. Whenever you feel hurt, be willing to look inside and get to the core of your pain. Remember, experiences outside of ourselves are a reflection of what is inside. When you feel pain, ask yourself, What is coming up for me? What is my soul trying to learn? Another person can love us, but first we have to love ourselves in order to recognize and receive love at the soul level.

Process your emotions. It is important to acknowledge, own and process your emotions. If you are sad, cry; if you are angry, let it out in writing or beat a plastic bat on a pillow. Find an outlet and give credence to your emotions. This is vital for your emotional, psychological and physical well being. If you avoid, deny or suppress your emotions, you will surely lose your way. Use your emotions as the guides and tools they are intended to be.

Consciously direct your focus. Focus on and be grateful for the qualities you love about yourself and your life. When you get into the habit of seeing the best in yourself and others, your relationships, and your life, will expand in beautiful and miraculous ways. We all thrive in an environment of acceptance, appreciation and love. We all wither in an environment of negativity, scorn and judgment. Lift yourself and others up and look for the positive in all situations.

Boundaries. Explore who you are and stay open to learning more about yourself. Be aware of what is true for you and be willing to express it. When we respect ourselves, we are better able to understand, articulate and establish healthy boundaries. We also are more capable of understanding and respecting the boundaries of those around us. It is foolish to believe once we manifest our beloved then two will be as one. We are all individuals. It is important to take responsibility for our own healing and lessons to be learned. We must continue to take responsibility for developing our potential and fulfilling our unique destinies. Clear, conscious boundaries assist us in maintaining respectful, uplifting and loving relationships.

Respect and honor. Do not take yourself or your loved ones for granted. Never assume someone else belongs to you. Respect and honor your body, mind, emotions and soul. It is an honor and a privilege to be living this life and to have the connections and relationships we have. When we choose to respect and honor ourselves, we naturally see through the eyes of love and can more easily respect and honor others.

Empower yourself and others. Competition and the desire to control others occur when you feel insecure, inferior or out of control. If you are afraid to praise, empower, or lift another up for fear they might leave, be willing to acknowledge and express your fear. Dare to tell the truth and cultivate greater intimacy with yourself and others. Praising yourself and others is nurturing and healing. Express admiration, appreciation and respect, and it will most certainly bring out the best in you and those around you.

Gratitude. Express gratitude daily for your wonderful attributes, soul lessons and opportunities. Be thankful for the little things as well as the big things. Gratitude is a magnet and naturally attracts love, prosperity and fulfillment. It also contributes to healthier bodies and minds. What we focus on expands. Be grateful, and you will attract even more to be grateful for!

Heartfelt listening. Everyone longs to be heard. Listen with your ears, heart and soul. When you listen and truly hear yourself, you can more effectively listen and truly hear others. Be present; be in the moment. Listen to more than the words being said; listen without thinking about what you are going to say in response. Do not interrupt or finish someone else's sentence (even if you know what they are going to say). Be patient and wait a moment before you respond. Release the need to be right, rescue or fix anything or anyone. When we are present and listen deeply to another, we hold space for them to be as they truly are. Heartfelt listening creates a safe and sacred space for deep connection, profound healing and true love.

Allow "space" in the relationship. Allow time and space for yourself and your beloved. Love with an open heart and an open hand. Create breathing room within yourself and in all of your relationships. Imagine this breathing room is the gentle breath of Spirit surrounding you always. In a healthy partnership, we are not dependant nor are we independent—we are interdependent. Complementary interdependence is like a dance. There is an ebb and flow that shifts and changes with the tides and times. This sacred space around you and your partner creates the opportunity to move and dance gracefully and freely.

Love and nurture yourself. Treat others the way you want to be treated and also treat yourself the way you want to be treated! Do the little things that make your own heart smile! When you learn to nurture and adore yourself, you create a certain dynamic and energy and you will find others begin to treat you the same way. By consciously choosing to reside in the place of love within, you naturally attract love and easily share it with others. When we tap into Self-love, miracles happen. Jesus healed others because He knew who He was. Jesus was the son of God and an heir to the Universe. The essence of Jesus is love and so are you!

Take care of your Inner Child. Continue to be cognizant and conscious of your Inner Child. Honor the young and joy-filled aspect of yourself. Take the time to check in to see what your Inner Child needs and what makes them happy. Remember this is your true essence and you cannot be whole, happy or fulfilled without your child!

Curiosity. Never assume you fully and completely know yourself or your beloved. Each of us is an aspect of the infinite and there will always be more layers to explore. By cultivating curiosity, you keep the gateway open to new revelations—and fun! When we think we know all there is to know about someone, then the learning ceases and the fun subsides. Let curiosity inspire you to learn more about yourself and others. By cultivating a sense of awe and wonder, you create opportunities for joy, laughter, expansion and fun-filled discoveries.

Communicate with care. Do not be harsh or use hurtful words. Do not crush or discourage a loving connection with negativity. The words we speak leave permanent and indelible traces on our hearts and on the hearts of others. We can always find a gentle way to articulate even the greatest of frustration. Encourage rather than discourage. Do not criticize or demean. Choose language responsibly and carefully. Take a moment to consult with your heart before allowing angry, disempowering or vindictive words to fly from your mouth.

Friendship. The foundation of any lasting love relationship is friendship. Passion and attraction are nice qualities and ones that are wonderful to have in a committed partnership, but these qualities are bound to dissipate over time without the bedrock of friendship and trust. In a true friendship, we focus on seeing the best in each other. We fully accept one other and lift each other up. Once we become a true friend to ourselves, we can then be a true friend to others; we will also attract those who will have the capacity and desire to be our true friends!

Give and receive graciously. We cannot give what we cannot receive. We must also believe we deserve what we want before it can show up in our lives. Open your heart and mind to receive compliments, kindness and love from yourself and others. When we open up in our ability to receive graciously, we expand in our capacity to give naturally and easily. Give with an open heart and an open hand. Tithing is powerful process and sets energy and abundance into motion. Set an intention to tithe energetically and watch the universe give back to you in wonderful and synchronistic ways. Remember giving and receiving are like breathing. Both inhaling and exhaling are necessary for a balanced, healthy and joy-filled life!

Have fun. Our journey here is supposed to be joyful and fun. See the humor in all things. Be willing to laugh at yourself and at life. Laughter has the power to heal and fun is what makes the journey worth taking! We all have an Inner Child that loves to play. Playing keeps us light, healthy and happy. Remembering to play and have fun keeps us open to awe, spontaneity, joy and wonder.

Set intentions. The universe was created from intention. You always have the ability and the opportunity to tap into the power of the universe by setting deliberate intentions. Remember that every day and with everything you do, you may invite, align and co-create with Spirit by using the extraordinary power of intention!

Patience and kindness. The *Bible* tells us love is patient and kind. Love is not envious nor does it brag. It is not proud or seek to have its own way. When we truly love, we are patient and kind. When we learn to be patient with ourselves, we are more patient with others. Life and love are a process—we are healthier and happier if we can implement and flow with the important and powerful qualities of patience and kindness.

When you manifest truly loving relationships, with yourself, Spirit and subsequently another human being, this love creates a positive ripple effect in the world. One small light can brighten up a very large and dark room. Every one of us is a spark of God and an integral part of the whole. When we remember, believe and live our lives with this understanding, we easily connect with others of like-mind. The energy and sacredness from these types of relationships can heal the world and bring new hope.

When you manifest your true love, it may or may not mean you and your beloved will dance together forever. Sometimes in a soul's quest for continued evolution, choices and paths may take you in different directions. This does not mean the partnership was not sacred. As long as you continue to live and breathe, you are a work in progress. However, when you develop a truly loving relationship with yourself, this work can feel more like play. When love yourself unconditionally, your "happily ever after" is with you wherever you go and in whatever you do.

People ask me all the time if I believe I will be with Steve forever. I cannot answer this question. I never want to take this relationship for granted or assume anything. For now I am grateful and honored to be on this path with him. I know for Steve and myself, it is our goal and intention to continue to support each other in our respective healing journeys. We are learning, growing and having great fun as we explore and express who we are—creative, unique and highly entertaining human beings. I believe the primary reason for a conscious committed partnership is to cultivate the sacred space for each of us to deepen in our personal connection with Spirit, ourselves and each others. This type of relationship provides an incredible portal for self-discovery and deeper Self-love. Ultimately, however, I realize my happiness is my responsibility, just as Steve's happiness is his.

Yes, we can live happily ever after, but only after we make the courageous, enlightening and exhilarating journey to discover the kingdom of heaven within. Once we cultivate this sacred space in our heart and soul, it is reflected back to us in our experiences, our relationships and in our lives. When we lovingly connect with ourselves and Spirit, we are able to manifest relationships filled with reverence, blessings and treasures beyond our greatest imagination and surpassing our wildest dreams.

Love one another but make not a bond of love:
Let it rather be a moving sea between the shores of your souls.
Fill each other's cup but drink not from one cup
Give one another of your bread but eat not from the same loaf.
Sing and dance together and be joyous,
but let each one of you be alone,
Even as the strings of a lute are alone though they
quiver with the same music.
Give your hearts, but not unto each others keeping.
For only the hand of Life can contain your hearts.
And stand together yet not too near together:
For the pillars of the temple stand apart,
And the oak tree and the cypress grow not in each other's shadow.

~ Kahlil Gibran

Reading List

I have mentioned many of these books throughout *Manifesting Love From the Inside Out*. They have been powerful catalysts and companions on my journey and I highly recommend them. I am in profound gratitude to the authors who have created these works and for the ripple effect of their wisdom and healing in the world.

A Course in Miracles. Farmingdale, New York: Foundation for Inner Peace, 1975.

Bradshaw, John. *Family Secrets*. New York: Bantam Books, 1995.

Bradshaw, John. *Healing the Shame that Binds You*. Deerfield Beach, Florida: Health Communications, Inc., 1988.

Borysenko, Joan Ph.D. *Fire in the Soul*. New York: Warner Books, 1993.

Borysenko, Joan Ph.D. *Guilt is the Teacher Love is the Lesson*. New York: Warner Books, Inc., 1990.

Campbell, Joseph, ed. *The Portable Jung*. New York: Penguin Books, 1971.

Capacchinoe, Lucia. *The Power of Your Other Hand*. Franklin Lakes, NJ: Career Press, Inc., 2001

Chopra,Deepak M.D. *The Path to Love*. New York: Three Rivers Press, 1997.

Cloud, Henry and John Townsend. *Boundaries*. Grand Rapids, Michigan: Zoncervan, 1992.

Dyer, Wayne. *The Power of Intention*. Carlsbad, California: Hay House, Inc., 2004.

Emoto, Masaur. *The Hidden Messages in Water.* Hillsboro, Oregon: Beyond Words Publishing, Inc., 2001.

Fontana, David PhD. *Teach Yourself to Dream.* San Francisco: Chronicle Books, 1997.

Hanh, Thich Nhat. *The Miracle of Mindfulness! A Manual of Meditation.* Boston: Beacon Press, 1976.

Hawkins, David R. M.D. Ph. D. *Power Verses Force.* Carlsbad, California: Hay House, Inc., 1995.

Hawkins, Dr. David. *When Pleasing Others is Hurting You.* Eugene Oregon: Harvest House Publishers, 2004.

Hicks, Esther and Jerry. *Ask and it is Given.* Carlsbad, California: Hay House, Inc., 2004.

Hicks, Esther and Jerry. *The Amazing Power of Deliberate Intention.* Carlsbad, California: Hay House, Inc., 2006.

Holmes, Ernest. *Science of Mind.* Radford, Virgina: Wilder Publications, 2007.

Johnson, Robert. *She—Understanding Feminine Psychology.* New York: Harper Row Publishers, Inc.,1989.

Johnson, Robert. *He—Understanding Masculine Psychology.* New York: Harper Row Publishers Inc.,1989.

Jung, Carl G. *Man and His Symbols.* New York: Doubleday, 1964.

Keating, Thomas. *Open Mind, Open Heart: The Contemplative Dimension of the Gospel.* Amity House Press, New York: 1986.

Kubler-Ross, Elisabeth and David. *On Grief and Grieving.* New York: Simon and Schuster, 2005.

If you would like to contact the author, have questions, comments or would like to share your Manifesting Love story please go to www.ManifestingLove.net.